BIBLE TRUTHS
LEARNED FROM LIFE

BY
GAILEN (BUTCH) ABBETT

PRESS

DEDICATION

This book is lovingly dedicated to Margie, my wife, companion and friend; second only to Christ Himself in the impact she has had on my life!

CONTENTS

INTRODUCTION

The earthly ministry of the Lord Jesus Christ lasted a remarkably short time; no more than three and a half years. And yet Christ knew that He needed to impart many heavenly truths to His earthly followers in a way that they could understand and retain. To do this He used parables. A parable is a story that is fictitious, or imagined, (though it could easily have happened), whose purpose is to allow the listener to understand a teaching that is absolutely true. Jesus saw the need to use parables so often in His teaching that the Bible says this: "And with many such parables spake He the Word unto them, as they were able to hear it, but without a parable spake He not unto them: and when they were alone, He expounded all things to His disciples." (Mark 4: 33-34)

Ever since the very earliest days of preaching God's messengers have followed Christ's example and have used parables or helpful stories to get Bible truths across to the listeners. Throughout the centuries some of the greatest preachers of the Word have been masterful story tellers as they helped the general public to look into the heavenlies and see Bible truths as God intended them to be seen.

The great Welsh Baptist preacher, Ivor Powell, known affectionately as "The Man From Wales" often said that a good illustration or story was like a window which let in light. Sometimes the teaching of a Bible passage might remain somewhat dark and unclear, but a well chosen illustration or story could allow light to be shed on the passage, with the meaning becoming clear and comprehensible.

Of such is the nature and intent of this book. During the nearly 37 years my wife and I served as missionaries in France involved in Church work, I could not help but come across many true and amazing stories from Europe. Apart from three of these stores that come from personal observation, every story was found in print in some fashion; in ancient books, archives, periodicals and other papers.

The finding and setting aside of these stories took several years, as they were simply filed in a folder and left setting on a shelf in my office. When I felt the time had come to do something with this material, but having little time to devote to this endeavor, it took another 4 years or so in their writing. It has been a long and arduous road, but an agreeable one.

The important thing about reading is the learning. We read to learn, to dream, to imagine. We need to be inspired, to be taught, to be bettered. That is why this humble little volume seeks to put the emphasis on "Bible Truths". It is through God's Word alone that we can be inspired, or instructed, or bettered. These true stores are only there to act as windows of light, allowing us to see and understand a little better certain Bible passages, for they alone can change us from what we were, help us with what we are, and move us forward to what we can be, in Christ!

Gailen (Butch) Abbett

WHAT IS FAITH?

All of Paris was turning out for this event which promised to be a magnificent and glorious spectacle, even for the "City of Lights". Napoleon was giving public inspection of his troops. His Personal Guard would be there, along with all his major officers. Store keepers deserted their shops, office workers filed out into the streets, as every inch of space was taken by the myriads wishing to catch a glimpse of their Emperor and his Grand Army. The army waited in perfect attention on the place of the Carrousel, with the Louvre Palace to their backs, and the Tuileries Gardens before them. To their left flowed the Seine River, and to their right was the Royal Palace itself. The Emperor approached and began his inspection. Everything had to be perfect. His horse pranced and held his head high with as

much pride as the Emperor himself. Then, something caught the Emperor's eye. As he sought to stop
and give an order the reins slipped from his grasp
and the horse began to charge uncontrollably across
the Square, the Emperor unable to reach the flying
reins.

A simple soldier, seeing what was happening,
bolted from the ranks, jumped in front of the frightened horse, and was able to bring it to a halt. The
breathless young man stood sharply to attention as he
silently handed the reins back to his Emperor.

—Thank you...Captain! said the Emperor,
simply.

—In which regiment, Sir? asked the young
soldier, still wondering if he had heard correctly.
Pleased in the confidence he saw in this young soldier,
Napoleon responded: "In my personal Guard!" as he
turned and rode away. Seeing a group of high ranking
officers standing nearby the newly promoted Captain
approached them.

—What are you doing here? demanded a General
in no uncertain terms.

—I am a Captain of the Guard, Sir! came the
reply.

—What? Why you are a fool!

—He is the one that just told me so, Sir! responded the young soldier, pointing towards the Emperor who could still be seen across the Square.

—I beg your pardon, Captain! said the General. I was not aware of that!

This simple soldier took his Emperor at his word. He believed every word the Emperor said to him, in a faith that was simple, yet firm. Napoleon was hardly infallible, but God certainly is. We can trust His every word, and count on it as a fact. Faith is taking God at His word, and believing in it with all our hearts. It is standing on His promises. God is pleased at seeing the confidence we place in Him and His Word, and He stands ready to bless those who do so. Faith is not doubting what God has said, but knowing that God will do exactly what He said. We must then act according to those promises. How important is faith? Hebrews 11:6 tell us: "But without faith it is impossible to please Him; for he that cometh to God must believe that He is, and that He is a rewarder of them that diligently seek Him."

The Christian faith is not a "blind faith" as some skeptics might call it, for some people see only with their eyes, while others see with their hearts. Just as this young soldier had nothing more to hang his faith on than the word of his Emperor, may we never doubt the word and direction of our Saviour. Our faith in Christ must be unwavering, unchanging, and unstoppable!

THE OLD CONTEMPTIBLES

World War I was looming heavily on the horizon and tension was mounting to a feverish pitch between Germany and Western Europe, in particular with England. German leaders had historically held little respect for the British. Prince Otto Von Bismarck, Prussian statesman and architect of the unification of the German states, was once asked what he would do if England were to land an army on German shores. He replied that he would simply call out the German police to have them arrested.

This antagonism towards the British continued into the outbreak of World War I. The original British Expeditionary Force (B.E.F.), composed of 160,000 men, was sent into France and Belgium under the command of General Sir John French. It has been said that the German Emperor, Kaiser William II, sent an army order to General Alexander Von Kluck ordering him: "to exterminate first the treacherous British, and to walk over General French's contempt-ible little army."

A "contemptible little army" were they? Is that what the Germans thought of them? Because of this slanderous reference to them, from that time on these men were known as The Old Contemptibles. How did French's men react to this calamitous description? Were they offended? Hardly! Much to the Kaiser's surprise, they took it as a compliment! They adopted this nickname for themselves and wore it with pride. It was like a badge of honor as they marched into battle against their haughty and disrespectful foe. It is not necessarily a good thing for the enemy to think too highly of us. The Christians of the early Church understood this as they fought Satan and his henchmen on every market place, and every street corner where the Gospel was preached. The Bible was their Sword, and the Truth their shield. Marching into battle they were criticized, tortured, beaten, maligned and killed, which they accepted with joy:

"And when they had called the apostles, and beaten them, they commanded that they should not speak in the name of Jesus, and let them go. And they departed from the presence of the council, rejoicing that they were counted worthy to suffer shame for His name." (Acts 5:40-41) The early Christians were held in contempt by the world, as was Christ Himself. They were "despised and rejected of men" just as was the Saviour, which they accepted gladly for the cause of Christ, just as should every born again believer of Christ today.

They also received a name: "And the disciples were called Christians first in Antioch." (Acts 11:26) Yes, Christians! They would be called Christians, which means to be like Christ! But this term was not always meant as a compliment in those early days of the Church. After all, for many people of those days Jesus Christ was no more than that "insurrectionist" that was crucified between two thieves at Jerusalem. How did the disciples take that term sometimes given in derision? Just as we should today, with honor and pride! Honored to be saved by the grace of God, honored to carry forth the name of Christ into the battles of life, for we too can say: "And His banner over me was love!"

It is a terrible thing when some people dishonor the name they carry that is supposed to define who they are, such as a soldier that dishonors his uniform or the flag under which he serves. Or a policeman that brings dishonor to his badge and fellow officers, or a judge that offers dishonest judgments. May every true born again Christian walk worthy of that High and Holy Name, of Christ!

THE LESSON OF A
BROKEN VASE

Certain names from history will most likely remain in our memories as long as man can remember. Politicians, military leaders, emperors, scientists, explorers and musicians have all left their mark on humanity and history. But who would remember a potter? Yes, a simple potter! Names such as Churchill, Wellington, Dickens or Mozart come quickly to mind, but who would remember Josiah Wedgwood, (1730-1795)? You see, Wedgwood was not just a potter...he was a master potter! Born in Burslem, England to a family of potters, young Josiah was obligated to ply his trade with great seriousness after the death of his Father. Josiah was only 9 years old at the time, but devoted his life to the art of pottery making, and developed a large reputation. So much so that Charlotte Sophia, wife of King George III, made him the official royal supplier of dinnerware to the royal family. His fame and fortune were made. Moving his facilities to Stoke-on-Trent, his reputation and business flourished.

One day a certain British nobleman wished to visit Wedgwood's facilities, so a young assistant was assigned to show him everything he wished to see. Though this nobleman was seemingly quite cultured and highly educated, he gave proof of having a terribly filthy language. His mouth was a veritable geyser of profanity as the name of God was taken in vain and the Bible ridiculed. The young assistant was shocked by all this...at first. But as the visit continued he was found to slowly begin to laugh and take part in this debasing demeanor. Wedgwood saw this, and was extremely irritated.

Before taking his leave the nobleman wished to purchase a vase for his manor. An exceptionally beautiful and expensive vase caught his eye. Wedgwood held it in his hands and explained that it took many, many hours of hard labor to produce such a vase.

As the nobleman nodded in understanding Wedgwood sent the vase crashing to the floor, shattering it into a thousand pieces. The nobleman exploded: "But that was the very one I wanted, and you have destroyed it by your clumsiness," he said!

Looking him straight in the eyes, and responding with all the pent-up fire of a potter's kiln, Wedgwood replied: "Sir, there are things far more precious than a simple vase...things that can never be remade nor restored once they are broken. I can make another vase, but you can never render to my young assistant the pure heart he had before he was dirtied by your filthy language, and depraved tongue!" Somewhere along the way Josiah Wedgwood seemed to have learned the lesson of Matthew 12:34, "For out of the abundance of the heart the mouth speaketh". The problem is not so much the tongue, but the heart that waggles it, revealing to all the world the deplorable nature of that heart.

God says it this way in Ephesians 4:29, "Let no corrupt communication proceed out of your mouth, but that which is good to the use of edifying, that it may minister grace unto the hearers." According to this verse, a clean language edifies and ministers grace to those that hear it. That cannot be said of foul language.

Notice Colossians 3:8, "But now ye also put off all these; anger, wrath, malice, blasphemy, filthy communication out of your mouth!" We should notice that this is a direct order from God, and not a simple suggestion. God wants our language cleaned up and bad language out, completely and totally. Our words can build up, or they can destroy! It is up to us to decide. When the heart has been changed, it will be evident by the language we use.

KILLED IN AN AMBULANCE

It should never have happened. Ambulances are meant to save lives, not lose them. But that day along a small, twisting road in eastern France, the ambulance took Anna O. to her death. It was supposed to be a simple visit for the 80 year old lady to see her Doctor at Toul. Because of her age and feeble condition a private ambulance was dispatched to carry her to and from the appointment. Everything went well until the return trip. At an intersection known for its numerous accidents, a right of way was not respected, and the collision with another vehicle was horrendous.

In the violence of the collision the ambulance became airborne, did a complete roll over, and came crashing down on its four wheels. The back door had flown open and the elderly patient was flung from the ambulance along with the bed upon which she was resting. She was killed upon impact. When she took her place in that ambulance earlier that day Anna never dreamed it would become a vehicle of death. She had put her faith and trust in that ambulance, only to lose her life tragically.

We cannot help but put our faith and trust in people and things every day of our lives. We trust our automobile to not break down on us, we trust other drivers to not run into us, and we trust even a simple chair to hold us up when we set down. We exercise our faith time after time, and most of the time we are rewarded for it. But not always! It can sometimes be tragic, such as in the case of Anna and the ambulance. Remember Absalom? This rebellious son of David was used to riding a mule instead of a horse. It was more sure footed and untiring in getting him to and from battle. But one fateful day as Absalom was fleeing in defeat, his faithful mule took him under the thick boughs of a great oak, where Absalom's long hair became caught up in the dense branches of that tree. II Samuel 18:9 says: ..."and he was taken up between the heaven and the earth; and the mule that was under him went away." He was betrayed and killed by his formerly faithful mule.

Many people today are doing the same thing in a spiritual sense. They are putting their faith and trust in a Church, in a religious system, or even in the folly of following a man. In doing so they run the huge risk of being shipwrecked along with the ship. Bad doctrine and unscriptural beliefs cannot save, no matter who might be the one promoting them, and no matter how big the crowds. Some churches will urge you to put your faith in sacraments, and manmade rituals. "Trust us, they will say, and we will get you to heaven!" Yet Jesus said in John 14:6: "I am the way, the truth, and the life: no man commeth unto the Father, but by me."

How great is our need today to be careful about who we follow! Jesus Christ and Him alone, that is the only way to Heaven. Don't put your trust in a false, floundering and even deadly religious ambulance. Ask yourself on every issue: "What does the Bible say?" Should you be in a place or under religious leadership that is in direct conflict with the clear teaching of the Scriptures, then look elsewhere. There are good places and good people that will work with you and walk with you in your Christian life. Don't ride a misdirected and tragic ambulance to a Christless hell. Put your faith today in the finished work of Christ on the cross!

A WHITE WALL
FOR THE WIDOW

There comes a time in our lives when we all need some form of protection, from some one, or from something. We often need a wall of defense behind which we can find safety and security. God reminds us that He wishes to provide that wall of defense for those that will put their trust in Him. Psalm 125:2 tells us: "As the mountains are round about Jerusalem, so the Lord is round about His people from henceforth even for ever." Those mountains are mighty and majestic, and they are the type of walls we prefer to have about us. But God does not always need might and power to protect His people. He can do so with something as light and fragile as a snowflake. The following true story will illustrate that fact.

January, 1814 saw war raging across most of central Europe as Swedes, Cossacks, Germans and Russians all fought for control of vast territories of land. The Cossacks were perhaps the most ruthless as they often fought as mercenaries for the Russian government, being used to expand the Russian frontier, which allowed them to plunder, sack, and ravage their way through all new lands conquered. On January 5, 1814 they stood outside Selswick, a small town in central Europe, waiting for a temporary truce to terminate at midnight, giving them the freedom to burst in chaos upon the helpless inhabitants of the town. On the outskirts of this town stood a house inhabited by an elderly widow, with her daughter, who was also a widow, and a grandson of 20 years of age. Knowing the truce was about to end and that danger would soon be at her door, the elderly lady raised up a prayer to God that He would build a wall about them to protect them from the enemy. The grandson scoffed at this feeble prayer. How could God or anyone else avoid the inevitable and stop the invading army from doing as it wished? "Do you think that if it were the will of God to build a wall around us, it would be impossible to Him?" she replied. Even before the midnight hour was struck the invading Cossack ruffians could be heard coming into town. In loud, boisterous tones they went from house to house, asking for nothing and taking what they wished. The incessant tramp of horses' feet and the ribald voices of plunderers could be heard on every side, but no one came to the bolted front door of the widow's cottage. The hours passed away and little by little the invading swarm could be heard moving on to new conquests. In the shuttered quiet of the widow's refuge none dared to break the silence. Huddled together they awaited the morning light, and wondered: Why, why had the Cossack armies not come to their defenseless door? Or, had they really been defenseless?

Calm reigned over the early morning light as the widow and her two companions stepped fearfully into the driven snow outside their house, and discovered the means by which the Lord had saved them. Snow had fallen furiously on that January 5. The great winds of the blizzard had driven the snow into drifts taller than a man, between the house and the road. Apparently the Cossacks were tired, cold and hungry and decided to push on looking for easier prey rather than brave the work it would have taken to enter into that humble house. God had erected a wall of white in response to the widow's prayers.

Yes, God can use a mountain to protect His children, should He so chose, or He can use something as fragile as a snowflake. We must remember that God loves us and wants to protect His children, but the important thing is not the tool being used, but rather the Hand in which it is held! Put your trust in that Hand!

MAX WILL NEVER MAKE IT TO HEAVEN

Before me on my desk at this moment is a most remarkable photograph taken during World War Two, showing nine allied soldiers standing in three rows of three, in a German prisoner of war camp named Colditz. The remarkable part of this story is that one of those men is not a man at all. He is Max, and he doesn't even exist. We will come to his story in a moment.

Not just anybody was sent to Colditz, for it was founded to house prisoners that had made at least 3 or 4 attempts to escape from other prisons. Housing over 600 men, hundreds of attempts had been made to escape from this high security prison, and only 26 had succeeded: 12 Frenchmen, 6 Dutchmen, 7

British, and one Polish man. This fortified castle built in the 17th century by Augustus the Strong, King of Poland, was an impressive rock structure dominating the Mulde River below.

In spite of the great danger the Allied men were very ingenuous in seeking ways of escape. Handmade tools were able to unlock nearly any door in the prison. Soldiers listened secretly to the BBC on a radio they had made by hand, and when it was found and confiscated by the Germans, at least two more were already waiting to take its place. One of the most gifted men in making something out of nothing was Frédéric Guigues, who, when visiting Colditz prison 20 years after the war, looked in his old hiding place, and there was his makeshift tool-box, still undiscovered after all those years.

This brings us back to the story of Max. The Dutch men in Colditz realized that it was not enough to find a way to escape; for they must find a way for the escaped fellow to be accounted for in the daily roll-call or the chase to find him would be quickly under way. So these men of great artistic talent carefully constructed a dummy to resemble the average soldier. Knowing they would be called to roll-call by rows of three by three they placed Max in the middle position where his lower members were well shielded by those around him. There was always someone in the back ranks to respond when the name of the missing soldier was called out. Held up by the men walking beside him Max moved and swayed so realistically with this tight knit group of 9 men that never once in the 6 years of the war was Max found out.

Unfortunately many people are like Max. They aren't true Christians in the Bible sense of the word, but they try to act like one. They have never been "born again" but they know how to talk like a Christian, how to walk and act like one, so they feel they can somehow pass that great "roll-call" in eternity when only the names of God's children will be called out. Jesus warns us of the folly of such false hopes as He tells us in Matthew 7: 21 & 23: "Not every one that saith unto me, Lord, Lord, shall enter into the kingdom of heaven; but he that doeth the will of my Father which is in heaven. — And then will I profess unto them, I never knew you: depart from me, ye that work iniquity." No, Max could never make it to heaven, for he was not real. Are you for real? Come to Christ in repentance and salvation, and hear the Father call out your name in Glory. No imitators will pass that roll-call!

JUST AS I AM: PART ONE
In the Garden of Decision

66 **J**ust as I am, without one plea, but that Thy
blood was shed for me,

And that Thou bidd'st me come to Thee, O Lamb
of God, I come, I come!"

There was a time in my young Christian life
when I had begun to tire of the grand old invitational
hymn, "Just as I Am"! I had nothing against it, you
understand, but I felt somewhat worn out on it as it
seemed no other hymn was played as often during
times of invitation during Church services. God, in
His infinite grace and goodness towards me did not
leave me in my languid disillusion on the subject,
but brought me instead into contact with the remarkable research on this hymn done by Frank Boreham,
the outstanding Baptist pastor-missionary-writer-

researcher, par excellence. "Just as I Am" has never again been the same for me. It has taken on new life. I began to see it as God meant it to be, and I now await its tender refrain with anticipation. To learn the story behind this touching hymn I must ask you to go with me to Grove House in London, the home of Charlotte Elliott. The date is May, 1822.

Charlotte's family is a staunch part of their Evangelical Anglican Church. God and His Church dominated the very fiber of the Elliott home. Her brother began a ministry in the city of Brighton that has left its mark until this day. Every member of the family lived for the cause of Christ, except Charlotte. She could always be found in Church, there on the pew beside her loved ones, but she could not share their enthusiasm or joy. Charlotte had no problem with the Church. Her problem was herself. When she looked upon the things of God she could only see holiness and purity. When looking upon herself she could only see her sins and great unworthiness. She felt she could not come to God. He In the Garden of Decision could not possibly want to save a sinner such as she!

That is when God stepped in on this glorious day in May, 1822, when Charlotte is now 33 years old. Dr. Caesar Malan, the powerful preacher from Geneva, Switzerland is preaching in London and has been asked by the Elliott family to share their home during this time. It took little time for Dr. Malan to notice the battle raging within the soul of Charlotte. His heart was burdened to find the way to point her to Christ. After several days in the Elliott home he spoke softly one day to Charlotte about her soul, only to be gruffly turned away. Being troubled in her conscience about the way she had treated their illustrious guest, Charlotte approached Dr. Malan a few days later to apologize.

"I have been thinking a great deal of what you said, she added. I feel that I should very much like to come to Christ; but I don't know how!"

"My dear young lady, Dr. Malan replied, you need worry no more about that! Come to Him just as you are!"

"Just as I am? Just as I am?" she thought. That is how God wants me to come?"

In those simple words, taken from John 6:37, Charlotte saw daylight break into her troubled and darkened heart: "All that the Father giveth me shall come to me; and him that cometh to me I will in no wise cast out." That verse brought the light Charlotte needed, providing for the true birth of her soul. She managed to look beyond her sins and saw the Saviour. No sin is too great to be forgiven.

But what about the birth of that song we spoke of? For that we will have to leave the garden of decision and journey into a valley of despair.

JUST AS I AM: PART TWO
In the Valley of Despair

66 **J**ust as I am, tho' tossed about. With many a conflict, many a doubt.

Fightings and fears within, without, O Lamb of God, I come, I come!"

We have just gone for a delightful walk with Charlotte Elliott as she journeyed through her "Garden of Decision" and found Jesus Christ as Saviour. Thanks to the Spirit led preacher from Geneva, Dr. Caesar Malan, Charlotte learned the great truth of John 6:37, *"All that the Father giveth me shall come to me; and him that cometh to me I will in no wise cast out",* as she came to Christ just as she was, in spite of herself depreciating image of herself. Charlotte came to Christ as any sinner must, that is, just as we are.

Two years after her garden experience Charlotte moved to live with her brother Henry and his family, at Brighton, where he was Pastor and founder/ director of a very unique school for young ladies. Charlotte's health continued to be quite weak, and it was of great consolation to her to be able to help Henry in his ministry, as her health permitted. There were many occasions however, when her health kept her shut-in at home while the rest of the family was busy in the Lord's service. This often brought on bouts of despondency for fragile Charlotte. Dark thoughts haunted her mind. Did God have nothing for her to do? Could God use such a frail creature as she? Charlotte had left that garden of decision for the dark and sinister valley of despair.

This soul-torture reached its climax one evening in 1834. Charlotte is now 45 years old and is alone at the house as her brother and his family are gone for the entire evening in ministerial matters. Almost too ill and despondent to move, Charlotte sank down in an old familiar chair before her writing desk. The weight of her doubts and fears seemed to crush her very heart and soul, but Charlotte was determined to get to the bottom of it all, and receive an answer from God. Her mind took her back to that garden experience years before when Dr. Malan helped her to see the truth she needed in John 6:37, the truth that God expects sinners to come to Him for salvation in true repentance, just as they are.

"Just as I am! she seemed to be repeating to herself. Just as I am! If God wanted me to come to Him for salvation just as I was then, then why would He not accept me today, just as I am, in spite of my weaknesses and poor health?"

The light of John 6:37 took on a new glow and meaning for her. Her heart took courage and her shoulders lifted from under the weight of doubt, as she reached for paper and quill to put her thoughts in writing. Her pen flowed easily as line after line ran from her heart to finger-tips, and the poem we know as the invitational hymn, "Just As I Am" came into being. When Charlotte's family returned home that evening she handed them the paper and found them immediately touched by the words, as millions have been since then. It was printed as a leaflet, anonymously at first, and was put into the hands of literally thousands of people. Yes, I must come to God "Just As I Am" in salvation, for there is nothing I can do in advance to prepare the way to God or to satisfy Him. I must also not forget to come to God "Just As I Am" with my life of service for Him, for He knows of what I am made. He knows my strengths and weaknesses, and wishes to take me just as I am, just as the Potter begins His work with the clay before a beautiful piece of pottery emerges!

One of those leaflets of Charlotte Elliott's powerful poem found its way into illustrious hands, and prepared a fragile soul for eternity. Let us read on!

JUST AS I AM:
PART THREE
In the Valley of the Shadow of Death

"Just as I am, Thou wilt receive. Wilt welcome, pardon, cleanse, relieve.

Because Thy promise I believe, O Lamb of God, I come, I come!"

We have learned much about John 6:37 from the life of Charlotte Elliott: *"All that the Father giveth me shall come to me; and him that cometh to me I will in no wise cast out"!* We saw her accept Christ as her Saviour thanks to that verse. We later saw God use that passage to help her see that He loved her and wanted to use her in His service in spite of her physical infirmities, just as He accepts each one of His children, just as we are, with our unavoidable weaknesses, *"For He knoweth our frame; He remem-bereth that we are dust". (Psalm 103:14)* But this twofold blessing from Scripture has a third partner in promise. To see this promise fulfilled we must go to Grasmere, Westmorland, to the home of the great English poet, William Wordsworth.

William Wordsworth, (1770-1850), was never sure of how to know God, feeling that God could be found everywhere in nature, as many of his earlier works will attest. He lived a life with few rules and regulations, finding little in life that could satisfy his searching heart. His close friendship with Coleridge helped, but there was still something missing. He still needed an answer. Sir Walter Scott, the Scottish poet and novelist provided that help. Wordsworth's Scottish friend was an ardent follower of the Lord Jesus Christ. In the garden of Scott's cottage at Lasswade you will find a sundial with this inscription engraved upon it: "The Night Cometh!" taken from John 9:4, the keynote verse of Sir Walter Scott's life: *"I must work the works of Him that sent me, while it is day: the night cometh, when no man can work."* William Wordsworth would never again be the same. From that time on it is said that his life and beliefs took on a form of conservative faith, unknown to him in his earlier years. His questions had been answered. He need seek no more!

We now find ourselves in Wordsworth's home in Grasmere, Westmorland. It is 1847, and Wordsworth's daughter, Dora, lay dying. She is only 43, and has been the treasure of his heart. "My one and matchless daughter!" as he tenderly referred to her. Wordsworth was a constant presence at his daughter's bedside, seeking to comfort and assure. One day an envelope arrived for Dora, and inside was a copy of Charlotte Elliott's poem, "Just As I Am". The effect was immediate. Dora brightened and said: "Why, that is the very thing for me!" Until her last day Dora would have this poem read to her ten or twelve times a day, often being read by the deep and trembling voice of her illustrious father. "And now, my hymn!" she would call out after finishing with some personal necessity. "The Lamb of God! The Lamb of God! Yes, I come! I come!" Dora went into eternity with the promise of God expressed in that poem, engraved upon her soul.

Three years later, on April 23, 1850, Wordsworth's own time had come to depart this world. "Is that you, Dora?" he was sometimes heard to call out, as if looking beyond those present and into the heavenlies.

And then, he was gone. Today the little cemetery at Grasmere holds the six tombstones of the Wordsworth family. On Dora's stone, beside her father's, you will find carved a lamb, and behind that lamb, a cross. A precious reminder that when I stand one day on the last step of this life, before the first step of eternity, God will take me then, as He has now, just as I am! In that day I too can say: "Oh Lamb of God, I come, I come!"

A CHRISTMAS CAROL IN NO-MAN'S LAND

The Franco-Prussian War of 1870 was in full swing. Thousands of soldiers from both sides were dying daily in this war of egos that lasted less than ten months. On one such battlefield over 6,000 soldiers died on one torridly hot August day, just outside a small Alsacien village. They fought from Alsace to Metz, to Sedan and to Paris until Napoleon III abdicated, paving the way for the Treaty of Frankfurt in May, 1871, bringing an awkward end to the conflict. These were dark days for all of Europe, but there were occasional glimpses of light. For example:

It is now Christmas eve, 1870 and armies from both sides of this war have been charging each other for days. Taking a respite from the slaughter to regain their forces, each side watched the other closely across the battle littered land between them. But it was Christmas eve, and neither side seemed to have the heart to fight on that nostalgic occasion, as thoughts turned more to home than in doing battle.

Suddenly, a young French soldier steps slowly from his ranks and advances into no-man's land. He stops on a small knoll facing the enemy. Several German marksmen draw their sights on him, their finger on the trigger ready to fire. But with a strong, clear voice the young soldier begins to sing a well known Christmas carol, as his voice rings out: "Noel, Noel, un Roi est ne en Israel". (Noel, Noel, a King is born in Israel) As the young soldier sings stanza after stanza of this touching Carol there is total silence from both sides of the battlefield. Weapons were laid aside for those few moments, and tears could be seen in the eyes of those whose hearts had been turned towards home. When the singer was done he turned calmly and rejoined his ranks. A long silence ensued as each one thought on what Christmas meant to him. Then a German soldier stepped from behind his fortifications and made his way to the place where the French soldier had stood. Raising his eyes to the heavens he began to sing in German the same Christmas carol. He sang each stanza loud and clear and when he got to the chorus both armies joined him in song; the one side singing: "Noel, Noel, Er ward geboren in Israel"; and the other side singing: "Noel, Noel, un Roi est ne en Israel". As the last words echoed across the valley the German soldier returned safely to his lines and the evening remained quiet as each one meditated on what had just transpired, and some bowed in humble adoration of the Christ Child.

Man has always been gifted at turning light to darkness, turning peace into war, and turning joy into sorrow. But God has always provided a Light to show us the way through the darkness. These soldiers caught a glimpse of that Light during the darkness of battle. Here is the Scripture passage that inspired that Christmas carol sung in no-man's land:

"For unto us a Child is born, unto us a son is given: and the government shall be upon His shoulder: and His name shall be called Wonderful, Counsellor, The might God, The everlasting Father, The Prince of Peace."
(Isaiah 9:6)

THE MONUMENT
NOBODY WANTED

It is cold and humid on this mid-winter day of January 27, 1887 as the workmen break ground in the frozen dirt of the grassy park known as the Champ-de-Mars, in the heart of downtown Paris. City Hall had decided that Paris needed a striking monument that would be the main attraction for the World's Fair to open at Paris in 1889. As many as 700 candidatures were submitted for this project, 18 finalists were retained, with one winner. But would this architect be a true winner? As soon as the first shovel of dirt was taken from Parisian soil an avalanche of criticism besieged City Hall.

It looked as if nobody wanted this monument. Tancrède Boniface, whose property bordered the

Champ-de-Mars filed a legal complaint in Court trying to stop the whole operation. Trees had to be removed from the public park causing an uproar from local residents. A certain professor in mechanical engineering warned City Hall and the public that after a certain height the monument would collapse like a house of cards. French writers and intellectuals also got into the act by circulating a petition to stop construction of this "monstrosity". Novelist Guy de Maupassant called it a "hideous skeleton". Writer Léon Bloy referred to it as a: "tragic lamp-stand".

Undaunted, the architect continued this project to which his name would forever be attached. Finally, on March 31, 1889 Gustave Eiffel climbed the last steps to the summit of his tower and raised a French flag measuring 7, 50 meters, by 4, 50 meters, saying that the French flag was the only one in the world to fly from a flagpole 300 meters in the air. It had taken Eiffel two years, two months and four days to complete his monumental task. Over two million five hundred thousand rivets were used to erect the Eiffel Tower, at a total cost to the city of Paris of 7,799,401 francs, and 31 cents. There was not one serious injury to be deplored during its construction. Therefore, on opening day of the World's Fair, Gustave Eiffel penned this note in the official register: "Ten minutes before noon, May 15, 1889. Opening of the Universal Exposition and the entrance of the public. At last!..."

It is hardly possible to compare the building of any monument to the coming to earth of the Lord Jesus Christ, and yet we cannot help but see a parallel in the way people think. There was a time when it seemed nobody wanted the Eiffel Tower; today it is the pride of Paris. Speaking of Jesus' coming the Bible says: *"He came unto His own, and His own received Him not." (John 1:11)* Or again: *"He is despised and rejected of men; a man of sorrows, and acquainted with grief: and we hid as it were our faces from Him; He was despised, and we esteemed Him not". (Isaiah 53:3)* Only the Creator Himself knew the importance of why Jesus came to earth, and as Jesus hung upon Calvary's tree only His Mother Mary and the apostle John were there to watch and weep. Fortunately there is coming a time when Jesus will be known as He should be, as we see in Philippians 2:10-11, *"That at the name of Jesus every knee should bow.....and that every tongue should confess that Jesus Christ is Lord!"* May we see clearly the true value and glory of Christ without delay, worshiping Him alone, and serving Him faithfully, now!

A THREE WAY SALVATION

It is a strange but inescapable fact that some people are destined to go through life without ever getting to know certain other people though they are quite close in many ways. Much like two trains running side by side on parallel tracks. Others however, seemed destined to be forever interwoven in a certain complicity. Such was the case of this young British fellow taking some holiday in the beautiful mountains of Scotland. His Father, Lord Randolph, was a leading member of the British government, and his Mother the daughter of a New York financier. But his blue-blooded background meant little that day as the lad decided to take a swim in one of Scotland's famous crystal clear lakes. Cramps set in and the young fellow was in serious trouble. It seemed as if all hope was lost. As he called out one last time in desperation a young Scottish lad heard his pleas and came to his rescue. Nearly losing his own life in the process the Scottish rescuer managed to make it to shore, saving the lad and beginning what would be a life long friendship between them.

The British lad never forgot what his Scottish rescuer had done for him. On a visit to Scotland to see his young friend he informed him that his family had decided to finance his studies in any University of his choosing, something unthinkable for this financially modest Scottish home. As the years went by the Scottish lad decided to go into medical training, and graduated with honors from Saint Mary's Medical Hospital of the University of London, all financed by his British friend's family. An excellent Doctor, he was drawn into medical research, where his brilliant mind sought ways to save the greatest number of lives possible. In 1928 he brought to the world a medicine that has benefited nearly all of us, penicillin. You would know this Scottish life saver and Doctor as Sir Alexander Fleming, (1881-1955).

During this time the young British chap was making quite a name for himself in becoming the foremost leader and statesman of the British Isles during the dark hours of World War Two. During a historic trip to meet with Franklin D. Roosevelt and Joseph Staline he came down with pneumonia, and once again his life was in jeopardy. An emergency call went out and once again Alexander Fleming had a chance to save the life of his British friend, as penicillin was rushed in and the life of Sir Winston Churchill was spared. What a great debt Winston Churchill owed to his Scottish friend, for he owed him his life, twice!

The salvation we have in Christ goes even one step further, for it is a three way salvation. Notice I Corinthians 1: 9-10, *"But we had the sentence of death in ourselves, that we should not trust in ourselves, but in God which raiseth the dead: Who delivered us from so great a death, and doth deliver: in Whom we trust that He will yet deliver us!"* Do you see in this passage the three ways in which God saves us? Let us look at them one by one, as we rejoice in what God hath done!

1. *"Who delivered us from so great a death"*...
— Delivered of all our sins when we came to Christ in repentance for salvation.

2. *"...and doth deliver"...*

— A daily deliverance as He delivers us from a wasted life and guides us along.

3. *"...in Whom we trust that He will yet deliver us"...*

— Delivered from the throes of death, and placed with Him in the Heavenlies.

BURNED ALIVE IN HER WEDDING DRESS

The streets of Paris were alive with activity that day as people hurried to the Place Maubert, on this 27th day of September, 1558. The clickety-clackety of heels upon the cobblestone streets drew attention to the public execution about to take place a short distance from the Notre Dame Cathedral.

—"Hurry, hurry, you won't want to miss this one!" said a running passerby to a lady in a doorway, as he hurried along.

—"Who is it this time?" she shouted out quickly.

—"A young heretic woman, he said over his shoulder as he continued to run. And they say she wants to go to the pillar in her wedding dress, and she isn't even married! She is a widow-woman! Can you imagine that?"

And so it was that one more person was added to the crowd that day to watch the public execution of Philippe de Lunz, a young Christian girl whose only crime was to not have belonged to the Church of Rome, and to have handed out Gospel literature on the streets of Paris. Philippe de Lunz was a young widow, her husband having been taken from her side by a violent fever in 1557, when she was only 22 years old. Facing the flaming pillar with courage and resolve she was granted her one last wish, to go to her death wearing her wedding dress, reminding her of her dear husband she was soon to find again. It also spoke of her heart that had been given to Christ, letting all the world know that she had been eternally wed to her Saviour!

Philippe de Lunz was only one of many Christians in those horrendous days to give their lives for the cause of Christ. The Place Maubert, on the beautiful Boulevard St. Germain, was the scene of many such executions. A printer was burned at the stake there for the sole crime of having printed Gospel literature.

A young missionary from Geneva, Switzerland, Thomas Saint-Paul, was also burned alive at this infamous public square for the same "crime", his Gospel literature being added to the burning faggots that took his life. Thousands more were to follow throughout France and much of Western Europe. Catherine de Medicis, wife to King Henri II, and Mother to King Charles IX, was regent of France under her son's reign. Fearing the increasing numbers of Protestants and Evangelicals she set out to remove this "threat" from the Kingdom. On August 24, 1572 began what is called the Saint Bartholomew's Day Massacre, which saw several thousand Protestants and Evangelicals die on that one day on the streets of Paris, starting a fire that spread to the furthermost corners of France, taking the lives of 100,000 people or more. Like Philippe de Lunz, their only "crime" was having belonged only to the Lord Jesus Christ!

How does the testimony of these martyred saints speak to us today? How does our testimony compare to those that were willing to go to the flaming stake for the Gospel's sake? How well they heeded the words of Christ Himself in Mark 8:38, as should we: *"Whosoever therefore shall be ashamed of me and of my words in this adulterous and sinful generation; of him also shall the Son of man be ashamed, when He cometh in the glory of His Father with the holy angels.*" We owe a debt to martyrs such as these, for they have handed down the Scriptures to our generation with burnt and bloodied hands, having given their all for the Saviour. As their very bodies lay smoldering in the fire, a sweet fragrance was mounting before the nostrils of God, who extended to them the martyr's crown! May we handle God's Word with a Holy Respect; may we face our future trials with a Holy Resolve; and may we wait in patience for that Holy Reunion!

A LESSON
LEARNED LATE

Few of us would need an introduction to the life and ministry of John Wesley, (1703-1791). We know he would rise every morning at 5 am for Bible study and prayer. We know he was an untiring and fervent preacher of the Gospel. We know he would average around 20 miles a day on horseback, going from village to village, preaching 4 or 5 times daily. It is estimated that he traveled over 300,000 miles in this way, preaching well over 42,000 sermons, with untold thousands coming to Christ. Wesley died at the age of 88, preaching until the last month of his exemplary life. Yes, we know much about John Wesley, but did you know that the most important lesson he ever learned came to him much later in life than you would expect? The following story will help to show us how well he learned that important lesson.

John Wesley had been preaching all day, going from town to town as was his custom. It was now late at night and his faithful horse was following a dark trail through a dense forest leading to the next village where Wesley hoped to preach the following morning. Half asleep in the saddle Wesley was jolted to his senses by a man jumping from the shadows, weapon in hand. "Halt! Your purse or your life!" he shouted, holding the reins to Wesley's horse firmly in his grip. But the emptied pockets of the weary traveler produced nothing of value. Plundering the meager baggage the bandit looked at Wesley and exclaimed: "Books! Nothing but books! What good are they?"

Wesley replied calmly: "I have something for you of great value, of a very great value. Believe me, if you do not believe this to be true now, the day will come when you will regret bitterly the life you now live. At that moment remember these words: *"The blood of Jesus Christ His Son cleanseth us from all sin!" (I John 1:7)*

Don't forget that, Wesley continued, for this will be your only hope!" With a grunt and a curse the man turned and disappeared into the darkness.

Years later, after an evening of preaching in a large city a man came forward, insisting on speaking with Wesley. "May God bless you Sir! he began. *"The blood of Jesus Christ His Son cleanseth us from all sin!"* was the message you gave me years ago. I was that thief that thought to rob you one night in the forest. That Bible verse you gave me followed me for many years until I fully understood the meaning, and I confessed my sins to the Saviour!" With tears in his eyes he thanked Wesley for having taught him that great lesson.

Wesley had learned that lesson well, but he learned it later than you might have expected. Wesley was ordained as a deacon in 1725 and began preaching almost immediately. He devoted his life to the ministry and even made a missions' trip to Georgia in the Colonies, but he returned home defeated and disillusioned. The missions' trip had been a disaster. He had no peace. Why? On May 14, 1738 Wesley attended a preaching service in the Aldersgate Street in London where he realized for the first time that he had never personally accepted Christ as his Saviour. He did so that night, and at the age of 35 his life and ministry were transformed. He learned this lesson rather late in life. Have we learned this lesson in good time? It is hardly possible to accept Christ too early in life, but you can wait until it is too late. You may be a Church member and even be extremely active in your Church, just as Wesley was in his, but just as Wesley you will one day return home your head down in defeat and emptiness. You too must be sure to have gone by way of the cross in true salvation in Christ, for this is a lesson that needs to be learned early in life!

FAKE GRAPES

S atan doesn't mind if people worship, as long as they do not worship the right person or object. Both Isaiah 14 and Ezekiel 28 show us that Satan longed for worship for himself in heaven, even wishing to overthrow God and sit upon His throne receiving the worship of all heavenly beings. Thrown from heaven in defeat Satan could not destroy man's penchant for worship, but he could misdirect it so that it would avail nothing. Hence, right from the gates of Eden man has fashioned himself gods made of wood and stone. Worshipping everything from cows to crocodiles he has turned his affections to that which can never satisfy nor help, rising from his knees chapped from humble adoration more empty than when he knelt, as Satan looks on in a smile of silent victory. God has not failed to warn us about this.

*"For the customs of the people are vain: for
one cutteth a tree out of the forest, the work of
the hands of the workman, with the axe. They
deck it with silver and with gold; they fasten
it with nails and with hammers, that it move
not. They are upright as the palm tree, but
speak not: they must needs be borne, because
they cannot go. Be not afraid of them; for
they cannot do evil, neither also is it in them
to do good." (Jeremiah 10:3-5)*

Satan can be viciously deceptive in making
an object seem worthy of worship. He is gifted at
making a lifeless object seem to have the ability
of offering life, bringing only death and decep-
tion. An example from history comes to mind of a
similar incident. Zeuxis, (late 5th century B.C.), was
one of the greatest painters of ancient Greece. Pliny
and other ancient writers spoke very highly of him,
describing his immense fame and recognition. But
Zeuxis had a rival for the affections of the people,
named Parrhasius.

Who was the better of the two? It could not be
decided, so a contest was agreed upon. They would
both paint a similar portrait, and then see which

painting was the most realistic. History tells us that Zeuxis painted the scene of a young boy holding high a beautiful bunch of grapes. Would it prove to be more beautiful and true to life than the one done by Parrhasius? The answer came and Zeuxis was declared the winner when birds were seen pecking at the grapes in his painting. So realistic were they that they seemed to offer a free and ready meal for these feathered grape thieves.

A faithful and fervent preacher of a few years ago had a sermon entitled: "All of Satan's Apples Have Worms!" and how right he was! The title says it all. Satan has nothing good to offer. Never! His idols are lifeless and silent, and his rewards are nonexistent. The loin- clothed pagan in his African hut, or the Frenchman in his fashionable suit strolling down the boulevards of Paris are equally lost if they are serving anybody or anything other than the true and living God, the Eternal God of Scriptures! Jeremiah 10:10 reminds us: *"But the Lord is the true God, He is the living God, and an everlasting King: at His wrath the earth shall tremble, and the nations shall not be able to abide His indignation."* If Satan's apples have worms you can be sure his idols have termites, which will one day turn to dust at your feet. Don't look down to an idol, but upwards to the heavens, and the Eternal God thereof!

HISTORY WOULD
HAVE TO WAIT

S criptures speak to us of the extreme importance of keeping a promise, and honoring a vow once given. We see this in Ecclesiastes 5: 4-5, *"When thou vowest a vow unto God, defer not to pay it; for He hath no pleasure in fools: pay that which thou hast vowed. Better is it that thou shouldest not vow, than that thou shouldest vow and not pay."* This passage speaks of paying that which we have promised to God, but it goes further than that and shows us God's disdain for those who do not keep their promises. On at least one such occasion history had to wait, while a young lady kept a vow she had made to her Mother.

It is a shame that so few people today would remember the name of Harriet Quimby, a most remarkable young lady. Born in 1875 to a family of farmers on the shores of Lake Michigan, Harriet was still young when her family migrated to San Francisco, where her sparkling beauty and sharp intelligence attracted much attention. Preferring journalism to the theater Harriet was soon offered a job writing for Leslie's Illustrated Weekly in New York where she would write more than 250 articles, taking her to Cuba, Egypt, Iceland, Mexico, and beyond. Independent and modern, Harriet was always seeking new frontiers to cross.

She found that last frontier while covering an air show in 1910: she would become America's very first female aviator, a private club exclusively reserved up until then for men only. The Wright brothers had started a flying school, but women were not allowed. Aviator John Moisant allowed her into his school, along with his own sister, Mathilde, beginning in July, 1911. Later that year license number 37 was awarded to Harriet Quimby, making her the first American female aviator in history. From air show to air show Harriet showed her agility and daring, yet she was not satisfied. She rarely was for long. She knew her next challenge, she would be the first woman to fly across the English Channel.

Arriving in France she is loaned a plane by the famous French aviator, Louis Bleriot. Originally planning on flying from Calais to Dover the weather remained absolutely miserable, making any such attempts impossible. Feeling she stood a better chance of making the flight from Dover to Calais, Harriet loaded the plane on a ferry and set out for England. At Dover the weather remained deplorable, until the bright, sunny morning of April 14, 1912. But there was a problem. It was a Sunday, and Harriet had promised her Mother that she would never fly on a Sunday. Argue as they might, a promise was a promise, and after all, she had made that promise to her Mother, and it was important to her to keep a promise made to dear Mother. Finally at 5:30 am, April 16, 1912 Harriet took off in a dense fog over the cliffs of Dover and made her way towards the shores of France, touching down one hour later in the fields outside of Hardelot. The event should have received first page coverage in papers around the world, but Harriet's exploit was eclipsed in the news that at the very moment she was landing in Normandy the Titanic was sinking in the icy waters of the North Atlantic. But Harriet Quimby did not miss her rendez-vous with history, for she will be remembered for her many qualities, not the least of which was when she made history wait, while she kept a promise to her Mother!

Reader friend, have you made a promise to your Mother that you have not kept; a promise you know you should keep? It is not too late. Keep that promise now, and somehow Mama will know, as they always seem to be able to do!

A CLASH OF GIANTS

None would dispute the fact that Leonardo da Vinci and Michelangelo were giants. And yet these two titans of their time had a clash that changed the world of art forever. Leonardo da Vinci, (1452-1519) was born a peasant's son in Vinci, near Florence, Italy. He became an apprentice to Andrea del Verrocchio in Florence and quickly gained the recognition of all who saw his early works. Da Vinci's, "The Last Supper" and the "Mona Lisa" will stand as two of the greatest works of art of all times.

Michelangelo de Lodovico Buonarroti (1475-1564) was born in Caprese, Italy, but soon left home for Florence, located on both sides of the beautiful Arno River, where he began to study under the greatest masters of his time. He will always be remembered for his work at St. Peter's Basilica, and the Sistine Chapel in Rome. His unforgettable statue of David has been deemed by most as the most exquisite stonework ever done. Florence appealed to his creative nature, as it did to Savonarola, Dante and Galileo.

Florence was soon to be the scene however of a dramatic clash between the aging Leonardo da Vinci and the young upstart Michelangelo. Da Vinci was the older, highly reputed master of Florence, and yet when sketches for the decorations of an important building in Florence were requested the demand did not go to da Vinci alone. Sketches submitted by Michelangelo were highly acclaimed, and word even reached da Vinci that he was getting too old to produce the kind of works that were once known of him. Jealousy set into the heart of da Vinci and to his dying days he was never able to get over this affront to his dignity and honor. He spent the remainder of his days clouded over by gloom and sorrow. When Francis I, King of France, asked him to come to France in 1516 he did so, never again to return to his beloved Italy, or to Florence, the home of his glorious past.

Jealousy! The greatest and the smallest, the richest and the poorest, the smartest and the simplest, have all succumbed to this horrible fiend we know as jealousy. How true it is that: *"Jealousy is the rage of a man!"* as we see in Proverbs 6:34; an uncontrollable rage that is capable of destroying all we hold precious. One man is jealous because another is promoted faster in an office than he. A soldier becomes jealous when stripes are awarded more quickly to someone else. An athlete tears the locker room apart when taken out of a game for a lesser known player. The politician relegated to the back pages of the newspapers is jealous of the one that took his place in the public's eye. And worst of all, one Christian, jealous of another Christian, when the other person was requested to serve in some Church capacity he thought reserved only for himself!

There is a way to defeat jealousy; it is to imitate the Lord Jesus Christ. We see this in Matthew 11:29, *"Take my yoke upon you, and learn of me; for I am meek and lowly in heart: and ye shall find rest unto your souls."* There was no speck of jealousy in Jesus. As we learn to imitate Him, we will find rest before God, within ourselves, and with those around us!

THE COURAGE OF THE TEEN-AGE QUEEN: PART ONE

Any person wishing to do a study on the Kings and Queens of the British Empire will find no shortage of information on the subject. Many volumes have been written about the Royal Monarchs of days gone by. Yet, one of the most courageous Queens of British history is often passed over with hardly a mention in the dusty annals of our libraries, for you see, Lady Jane Grey was only a youthful 17 years old when she was proclaimed Queen of the British Empire on that fateful day of July 10, 1553. She did not desire to be Queen. After all, she was only third in line to the throne and had no desire to ascend to such a lofty position. Political and religious storms took the young Protestant lady from the quiet shadows of anonymity which she preferred, and thrust her into the white heat of the public eye.

The British Empire was engaged in a political-religious war. Catholicism was used to reigning without opposition, but the insurgence of the Protestant and evangelical faith was making inroads into England that the church of Rome found unacceptable. Wanting to put a Protestant ruler on the throne, Lord Chamberlain John Dudley, Duke of Northumberland, arranged for the marriage of his son, Guildford, to Lady Jane Grey, then only 15 years old. Rallying his forces around him he proclaimed Jane Grey Queen of the British Empire on July 10, 1553. Jane was now 17 years old. She wept when she heard of her proclamation, for this was a charge she did not want. In her own words she said this: "The throne is not made for me, it belongs to Mary, (Tudor). The throne that you offer me is as a yoke that causes me to tremble, and weighs me down; and chains, though they be of gold, are they not still just as heavy?" Sadly, her heaviest chains were yet to come.

From the very beginning Jane Grey knew that Mary Tudor was the first in line to the British Throne. Mary was the daughter of Henry VIII and Catherine of Aragon, but when Henry divorced Catherine and married Anne Boleyn in 1533, Mary was declared "illegitimate" and ineligible for the throne. Her position as eventual heiress was restored in 1544. She eventually married Philip II of Spain, a devout Catholic. Mary would later restore Catholicism as the only acceptable church of the Kingdom, hence her sometimes surname, Mary the Catholic.

Mary revived the laws dealing with "heretics", other words, anyone not belonging to the church of Rome. Under Mary's reign many hundreds of Protestants and evangelicals, with other opponents to her throne would die the martyr's death, giving Mary the name she will carry with her forever, "Bloody Mary"!

After having reigned for only 9 days as Queen of the British Empire, Jane Grey handed over to Mary Tudor, the crown she had never wanted, and never sought.

Mary had her immediately arrested and placed in the infamous Tower of London. This is where we will next find our heroine.

THE COURAGE OF THE TEEN-AGE QUEEN: PART TWO

Let us return to the Tower of London and find there our young 17 year old heroine, Jane Grey. After only 9 days as Queen upon the throne of the British Empire she finds herself alone, so desperately alone. John Dudley, Duke of Northumberland, the one who had forced Jane to the British throne, seeing his own life endangered, begged clemency of Mary Tudor, renounced his Protestant faith, reverting to Catholicism. This was to no avail as Mary soaked her pride in vengeance, making Dudley one of the first of hundreds to die by her bidding. Mary wanted Jane's husband Guildford, Dudley's son, to be executed in public, keeping Jane's execution in private. Hearing the roar from the streets below Jane rushed to her cell window, only to see the blood splattered body of her husband being carried past in a cart. "Farewell, farewell dear husband, she cried out. For there goes only the vilest part of your being, the more nobler part is already in heaven. Soon I shall be with you there, and our union shall be eternal!"

What gave this teen-age lady the courage to go on, that sustained her, when heads were falling almost daily? There can be no doubt about it; it was her deep and sincere faith in God! May we once again allow Jane to speak for herself. On the eve of her own execution she wrote a letter to her sister, sending her a New Testament in Greek. Here are excerpts from that last letter: "I am sending you, my dear sister, a "Book", though it is not ornate nor covered with gold, its contents are more precious than the most precious stones.....If you will rule your life by this Book and its contents you will inherit riches that man cannot take from you, robbers cannot steal, and the moth cannot corrupt.....Always learn to die, abandon the world, renounce the devil, detest the flesh. May your only delight be in the Lord.....Concerning my death, rejoice as I am, for I shall soon be discharged of this corruption; for I know that in losing my mortal life I shall gain life immortal!.....Farewell dear sister, put your hope in God, who will help you.....Your loving sister, Jane!"

The next morning the men and women of the Tower of London were moved with emotion. Some were in tears, for it is February 12, 1554, the day of Jane Grey's execution. Even the chief executioner's hand trembled on the giant ax as he stood at attention, not wishing to do the job to which duty bound him. Two servant ladies helped Jane bare her neck and shoulders. The executioner knelt to one knee beside her and asked for her forgiveness for that which he was about to do, which she did immediately. Her soft, girlish voice could be heard in one last prayer as she placed herself upon the block: "Dear Lord, into Thy hands do I commit my spirit." With those words the ax fell, and Lady Jane Grey went out to the fulfillment of Revelation 2:10, "Fear none of those things which thou shalt suffer: behold, the devil shall cast some of you into prison, that ye may be tried; and ye shall have tribulation ten days: be thou faithful unto death, and I will give thee a crown of life." Could a more fitting passage of Scripture be found to describe the heart of God for those of His precious children who laid down their lives for the cause of Christ, as did this courageous teen-age Queen?

Shortly before her execution one of the guardians of the Tower asked Jane if she would inscribe something in a book she had given him. She wrote this: "Live, as if you should die daily. Die in such a way as to be able to live without ever dying.

The day of your death is of greater value than the day of your birth!"

THE FLAMING
CHRISTMAS TREE

The story is told of a young girl named Myriam who saved many lives one Christmas eve, thanks to a clear mind and much courage. She lived alone with her father high in the snow covered Alps, where he was the Station Master of a remote train station. Boxes of decorations came out of their hiding places as garlands, twinkling stars and brightly decorated balls found their way to the waiting branches of their Christmas tree. Myriam's father reached for his coat and reminded her that he had to make one last visit to the Train Station to make sure everything was safe and secure for the passage of the last train to pass through their village that evening.

Myriam worked on alone in decorating their humble tree until suddenly there was a huge rumble that shook the house. Hurrying outside she found that a giant boulder had broken loose from the mountainside and had come crashing down right in the middle of the train tracks, just this side of a tunnel. She knew the train her father went to care for would be flying out of that tunnel in just a few minutes. Coming out of the darkness of the tunnel the engineer could never see the boulder in time to stop. A disaster was imminent. May lives would be lost unless she could think of something that would warn the engineer in time to stop the train. Myriam had no lamp, but perhaps a fire set in the tracks would do. But where could she find any wood that would burn under this blanket of snow? Hurrying back to her home she looked feverishly about for something that would burn, but it had to be something that would catch fire quickly and burn brightly. Myriam saw nothing that fit that description, until her eye stopped on her lovely Christmas tree. Her decision was made in a split second.

Holding the tree tightly in her stubby fingers she made her way back to where the boulder was on the tracks. There, near the entrance to the tunnel, she pulled a box of matches from her pocket and struck the first match. A small branch leaped into flames. Another match brought more flames to life and soon the whole tree was crackling from the rising flames. Scampering to safety Myriam could only wait, and pray that she had done enough. A blast of the train's horn could be heard, and now she could see its light. And then, oh joy of joys, Myriam heard the wailing scream of the train's brakes as the steel giant edged out of the tunnel just a few feet away from Myriam's flaming Christmas tree. The engineer leaped from the train, immediately saw the huge boulder just beyond and realized what Myriam had done. The courage of this mountain lassie and a flaming Christmas tree saved many lives that sacred evening.

There is another tree that was set nearly 2,000 years ago on a hill called Calvary, and it has started a fire that will burn in the hearts and lives of all those that will look unto the Christ of that cross. After communing with Jesus on the Emmaus Road two disciples of Christ offered these thoughts: *"Did not our heart burn within us, while He talked with us by the way, and while He opened to us the Scriptures?"* *(Luke 24:32)* Turning to Christ in faith will light a fire in your heart of hope and salvation!

THE HANDS
OF THE MASTER

The young German composer Felix Mendelssohn, (1809-1847) was so excited he could hardly contain himself. He was impatiently making his way towards one of the biggest cathedrals in Germany. But it was not the cathedral that caused his heart to leap with anticipation; it was the new pipe organ that had just recently been installed there. Its beauty and magnificent tones had raptured all who had occasion to attend. He had to see for himself; he had to hear with his own ears. As Mendelssohn stepped through the massive wooden doors of the cathedral his heart jumped as he heard the organ being played. The cathedral organist was practicing, and much to his surprise Mendelssohn recognized the piece being played as one of his own. But the organist was struggling with it and having a terrible time in getting it right. It was not going well for him.

Making his way respectfully to the side of the organist he asked if he might be allowed to play a number on such a splendid instrument. The horrified organist replied: "Never! I am for the time being, the only person authorized to touch this organ!" Multiplied pleas were made in an effort to obtain his permission, but the organist remained inflexible. Mendelssohn turned to leave, his head down and his heart heavy. But no! He had to try one more time, so returning to the organist he pleaded once again all the more earnestly. Mendelssohn's persistence paid off as the organist finally accepted to allow the visitor a chance to play. Mendelssohn took his place on the bench, adjusted the organ to fit his needs, and his fingers began to fly across the keys. Now it was the organist's turn to stand amazed as music gushed forth as from a geyser, filling the cathedral with such rhapsody as had never before been heard within those stone walls.

When Mendelssohn's fingers finally came to rest and the cathedral organist refound his voice, he humbly asked: "But Sir, who are you?" The answer was equally simple: "I am Mendelssohn!" The organist stepped back in shock and embarrassment as he realized what he had nearly done in refusing the great Mendelssohn his simple and now understandable request. Mendelssohn was already known throughout Germany, though still young. He would go on to compose many compositions, performed around the world. He became the musical director for the city of Düsseldorf, the conductor of the Gewandhaus Orchestra in Leipzig, and he would be the musical director to King Frederick William IV of Prussia. The humbled organist now thought upon the one he had tried to turn away, and how glad he was to have finally accepted his demands.

What a difference it made when that instrument was placed in the hands of the master! And what a difference it makes when we see the importance of placing our lives into the hands of the Master, the Lord Jesus Christ! Proverbs 3:5-6 tells us: *"Trust in the Lord with all thine heart; and lean not unto thine own understanding. In all thy ways acknowledge Him, and He shall direct thy paths."* Our lives will never be in tune with heaven, will never bring rhapsody to the hearts and lives of those around us, until we allow the Master to take charge. He alone can bring happiness and harmony through the instruments He has made. The key to this spiritual symphony is "submission". Only as we are totally submitted into the Master's hands can He accomplish His magnificent work in us!

"BE THOU FAITHFUL UNTO DEATH"

O ur title for this study comes from Revelation 2:10 where we see these words given to the Church in Smyrna, which represents the age when persecution was rampant against the recently born Church. This charge is valid for all of us today: *"Be thou faithful unto death, and I will give thee a crown of life."* Being faithful until the end is something any child of God can do. It has nothing to do with our intellectual capacity, our physical ability, our financial stability, or a host of other human standards. Faithful! Anybody can do that, no matter what our lot in life may be. The greatest examples in the Bible or in Christian history have been of men and women that knew how to remain faithful.

In Joshua 14 we see the remarkable story of Caleb. In this chapter he comes before Joshua, reminding him of their many battles together for Israel, and for their God. In verse 7 Caleb reminds Joshua: *"Forty years old was I when Moses the servant of the Lord sent me from Kadesh-barnea to espy out the land; and I brought him word again as it was in mine heart"*. Now, after many years of battle, Caleb has a request for his friend Joshua, as he calls attention to his age: *"And now, lo, I am this day fourscore and five years old"*, *(verse 10)*. Is the old warrior ready to retire, ready to hang up sword and buckler for good? Hardly, for in verse 12 he makes petition of Joshua to launch into another monumental battle as he asked: *"Now therefore give me this mountain"!* At the age of 85 he was still looking for lands to conquer and victories to be won for his God and for his people! God is still looking today for Calebs who wish to be faithful until death. An example can be drawn from an incident in the life of Louis XIV, King of France, (1638-1715), who reigned for 72 years over his people, the longest reign of any monarch in European history. Known as the "Sun King" he ruled France with an iron hand, and yet inspired absolute devotion from his subjects, especially from the military. However, being afraid of certain subversive elements in Paris he dared not dwell there, so he built the now famous Palais de Versailles, and moved there permanently in 1682. On one particular day an old seasoned veteran of his army asked for a personal audience with the King. The old veteran waited nervously to be called in from the antechamber, for he knew that the time was coming for him to be forced into retirement, sending him to "Les Invalides", a large complex of buildings on the left bank of the Seine River in Paris, which also held the final home for up to 6000 army veterans.

He soon found himself standing before Louis XIV. Humbly, but with the dignity of an officer, he formulated his request; he did not wish to be "banished" to "Les Invalides", (which means, "the disabled ones"), wanting to continue to serve his King! Louis XIV did not seem to share the burden of his faithful officer.

—"But you are quite old, my dear Sir!" replied the King.

—"Sire, responded the officer, I am only three years older than your Majesty, and I should like to be able to serve you for at least twenty years more"!

This slightly disguised attempt at flattery so impressed the King that he granted the wish of his faithful servant, allowing him to remain in active duty. There is something about faithfulness that touches the heart of God! When death finally relieves us of our duties for our King, the Lord Jesus, and we find ourselves standing before God to be judged, we will be judged not for what we had in our hands, but what we had in our hearts, for there lies the source of faithfulness! Your health may be poor, you may have other great limitations in your life, but if you remain faithful to God, He will honor that!

THE NAME MAKES ALL THE DIFFERENCE

It could hardly be said that Pablo Picasso was poor, though we understand that his paintings and other works of art have brought in more money for his estate since his death than they did for him in his lifetime. But the Spanish artist, (1881-1973), so called master of cubism, never forgot his meager beginnings in life and was always happy to find a way to economize his earnings. For example, he found that after dining in a nice restaurant he could make a simple and hurried sketch on the tablecloth, leaving it with the owner of the establishment as payment for his meal, the owner being only too happy to have an original Picasso in his possession.

On one such occasion Picasso had dined satisfactorily in a fine restaurant. Once again he had drawn a hasty sketch on the tablecloth. When it came time to pay the bill the owner refused, saying that Picasso owed him nothing in return for his sketch on the tablecloth. Picasso graciously acknowledged this gesture from the proprietor and prepared to leave. But the owner stopped him before leaving the table and asked Picasso if he would not mind signing his name to his drawings. Seemingly offended, Picasso replied firmly: "Sir, I have paid for my meal, but I do not have any intention of purchasing the restaurant!"

Those sketches without the name of Picasso on them would have a limited value, but those same sketches with Picasso's signature to show the authenticity of their origin would have meant considerable wealth for the restaurant owner. The whole difference was in the name! This is true of all the great artists. A famous painting, even the Mona Lisa, is not considered of great value because of the materials used to make it, for they cost only a few cents. But the name at the bottom of the painting, there is the difference!

Through the centuries many men have wanted to save their countrymen or their home country itself. Some wanted to be saviors of mankind, but man will always fall short in that endeavor. Man cannot provide salvation for man. Only God can do that! Man can only point other men to Christ. All other attempts will fail. Why? This act of salvation is only of value if the right name is signed on the bottom line. But there was a time many years ago when Jesus-Christ wrote His name in blood on the decree of salvation offered by God the Father. Without that Name above all names, our hopes would have no value. Consider these passages of Scripture:

"Forasmuch as there is none like unto Thee, O Lord; Thou art great, and Thy name is great in might." (Jeremiah 10:6)

"But these are written, that ye might believe that Jesus is the Christ, the Son of God; and that believing ye might have life through His name." (John 20:31)

"Neither is there salvation in any other: for there is none other name under heaven given among men, whereby we must be saved." (Acts 4:12)

"Wherefore God also hath highly exalted Him, and given Him a name that is above every name: that at the name of Jesus every knee should bow, of things in heaven, and things in the earth, and things under the earth." (Philippians 2: 9-10)

A document, even duly signed must be accepted. Have you done so with the offer of peace and pardon that God has offered you, signed and sealed by Christ with His own blood, shed on the cross?

HURTING THE ONES YOU LOVE THE MOST

How could he have done that? How could he hurt Juliette, his wife of many years, the one he loved more than anyone else on earth? He was 83 and she was 79. They had lived in peace and love for many years in this small French town, until that fateful day when he killed her.

The day started like so many others. They were going out together, so like always he went into the garage and prepared to back the car out to where Juliette could climb in easily beside him. But what was that? There was a dull thump as the automobile jumped over an object behind it. Stepping from the car the elderly fellow discovered to his horror the legs of his dear wife protruding from under the back of the automobile. For whatever reason Juliette had stopped an instant as she passed behind the car. What followed was tragic. Help was summoned; she was rushed to the best hospital in the area, to no avail. On that terrible, tragic day he unwantingly killed the one person he loved more than anyone else in the world.

Sin is like that. We often think of the effects sin has on us, and we have a tendency to think that it affects only the one committing the sin, but we often forget that our sins also affect other people, often the very ones we love the most. No man is an island unto himself. When we sin it does hurt us, but it most assuredly will hurt many others as well. Even if we are caught in one of our sins and pay the price for it, we often think it stops there. But not necessarily so. When Korah led a revolt against Moses and Aaron, he was caught up in that sin and judged by God for it. Unfortunately it did not stop there, for in his rebellion he carried hundreds of other Israelites with him, and when the earth opened her mouth and swallowed up Korah, the Bible says in Numbers 16 that the earth also swallowed up all his men, their houses, and all that pertained unto them, as hundreds of people lost their lives on that fateful day.

We rarely think of the effects our sin will have on others. When a man begins drinking he doesn't think ahead to the days of wages being poured into a bottle, of lost jobs, ravished health, and children left in want of basic needs. A smoker doesn't see why his children have poorer health because of living in a blue smog inside the home. The adulterer closes his eyes to the destroyed lives, the crushed love, and the hurt that will not go away from the heart of a wife or child. Yes, like the old song says, sin will take you farther than you will want to go, and make you pay a price you will not want to pay, with those you love the most, often being called upon to pay the bill.

How can we avoid this tragedy? By following the example of Joshua as we read in Joshua 24:15, when he said: *"...as for me and my house, we will serve the Lord."* The secret to what Joshua did was that he did not abdicate his position as the spiritual leader of his family. He was the one that made the decision to follow the Lord, and to walk in His steps, avoiding sin like the plague, because sin is a plague that will infect all the family. He led by word, but he also led by example. That is a great example to follow, for our own sake, and for the sake of those we love the most.

HE WAS A THREAT
TO HITLER

It is no secret that Adolf Hitler was ambitious. His bloodthirsty plans for world domination would allow no opposition in any form. Human opposition would bring arrest and imprisonment. Hostile written materials would be confiscated, heaped into huge piles and burned, with the public as witness. So it was in 1933 when Hitler took full power in Germany and began one of his first such acts in the destruction of a book he considered dangerous for his Nazi regime. Every copy of this book that could be found in home, school, library or bookstore was brought to the public place and burned. What was this story and who was this fictitious character that caused Hitler to feel so threatened? Strangely enough it was not even the story of a man, but of a child. As a matter of fact, it was not even a human child, but that of a baby deer, named, Bambi!

There were two reasons why Hitler went to war against Bambi. The first was its author, Felix Salten, (1868-1945). Salten's real name was Sigmund Salzmann, an Austrian Jew, born in Budapest, Hungary. When Hitler invaded Austria, Salten took refuge in Switzerland where he died in 1945. It was in 1928 that he first published his story of Bambi, in Austria, under the original title: "Bambi, Eine Lebensgeschichte aus dem Walde", ("Bambi, The Story of a Life in the Forest"). It was an immediate success. It was soon thereafter presented to Walt Disney who made his famous feature length film of it, being first presented in London on August 8, 1942, and then opening in New York on August 13, 1942. It had to wait until three years after the end of the war to come out in France in 1948.

The other reason why Hitler was so set against the story of Bambi was that it was: "Too pacifying and softening, (or weakening) for children". It was a story of love, tenderness and compassion, while he was looking for a Germany of rugged strength of heart and mind with no place for weakness. There would be no place for tears of tenderness under his regime.

As I thought on the foolishness of Hitler I could not help but think of the foolishness of the world that has often felt threatened by the men and women of God that have taken the Gospel to the furthermost ends of the earth, following Pentecost. The Gospel story they carried in their bosom was a story of love and compassion, yet these humble messengers were often despised and rejected by men, and many were burned alive on the public place. Eleven of the twelve disciples were martyred. Peter was crucified upside down, his head towards the ground, and the once doubting Thomas is said to have been executed by being stuffed into a hollow log before being sawn in two. Even though John escaped martyrdom he did not escape suffering, as history tells us he survived being thrown into a vat of boiling oil before being cast away on the island prison of Patmos. How accurate are the Scriptures that tell us: *"They were stoned, they were sawn asunder, were tempted, were slain with the sword: they wandered about in sheepskins and goatskins; being destitute, afflicted, tormented; OF WHOM THE WORLD WAS NOT WORTHY!"* *(Hebrews 11:37-38)* Though greatly worthy in the eyes of God!

NO, THERE ISN'T ANYTHING ELSE

For several hours this snowy Saturday afternoon I had been giving out Gospel literature on the streets of a large town South-West of Paris. I would need to find a Church to attend the next morning, but try as I might, not a single Gospel preaching Church could be found for miles around. So I resigned myself to visiting the old main line Protestant Church there in the heart of that town. I still harbored hopes of receiving a blessing and going away refreshed. Here is how those hopes were sadly disappointed.

The Church was packed for the morning service, more than usual so they said, because of the special speaker who would be bringing the morning message. As the special speaker approached the pulpit I could not help but notice his very casual dress, more appropriate for a back yard family get together than for a Sunday morning service. I noticed he had no Bible in his hands. For over half an hour he spoke about the social work of the Church, but something was badly missing. It was the Gospel message of the Lord Jesus Christ. Never once did the speaker mention the name of Christ. Never once did he read a passage from the Bible, nor quote a passage, or even make reference to one. The subject of sin and souls, of heaven and hell, or of repentance and redemption never once came up. I couldn't help but wonder why.

After the service was over I finally found a quiet moment to speak with this fellow. Speaking to him quietly and softly of my distress at not hearing anything about the Scriptures or of Christ, I asked him if I had heard correctly. Was I not mistaken? As I slowly presented my thoughts the guest speaker was rapidly building up steam. Hardly able to contain his irritation and aggravation he bellowed out: "What? That's not all there is! There are other things one can talk about besides Christ, you know!" I reminded him of the great crowd that was there that morning, and of the primordial need of every person there; that of knowing personally Jesus-Christ as Lord and

Saviour, and their need to hear that in a clear and simple Bible message. His temperature gauge was reaching unparalleled heights, so I thanked him for taking the time to speak with me as I took my leave.

As I made my way home that afternoon I thought of three things. First of all I thought of how hard it is to get people into the House of God. Getting people into Church has become more and more difficult in recent years, and yet, there was a house that was full with a wonderful occasion to present the Gospel. An occasion that was lost that sunny morning. Secondly I thought of how sad it is for people to return home from Church without having anything that would help them, or change them for the better. So many people returned home that day in the same spiritual shape in which they had arrived, because of not hearing a life changing and salutary Gospel message. Lastly I thought of how terrible it is to have such a deep responsibility, and to fail in it.

I remembered what the apostle Paul said on this subject, when he tells us in I Corinthians 2:2, *"For I determined not to know any thing among you, save Jesus Christ, and Him crucified."* This does not mean that we do not have a heart for the poor and needy, but it does mean that we realize that their greatest need is salvation in Christ. While we are polishing our fire engine's bell, souls are going up in flames without Christ, While we are whisking the dust off of our diplomas, souls are dying without hearing the simple message of Christ. While we are putting the crease back in our three piece suits, souls are still dressed in spiritual rags, asking how to receive their robes of righteousness. No, my disillusioned preacher friend, apart from Jesus, there is nothing else!

A TREASURE TOO LATE

It often happens in life that something important arrives too late to do much good: an umbrella after the rains have stopped; free tickets to last night's ballgame; or a precious medication after the patient has died. This thought crossed my mind as I read the story of a courageous lady from the Bourgogne area South of Paris. She began court and legal battles in 1959 to prove her family's rights as true owners of one of the most prestigious pieces of property in Paris, going from 97-99 Ave. des Champs-Elysees to the equally famous Ave. George V, and housing the world famous restaurant, le Fouquet's.

The problems began in November 1865 at the passing away of the Countess Coetlogon, the owner of the property. Joseph-Paul Mauprivez became the legal owner, but from that point on the legal waters became somewhat murky. Few legal documents could be furnished to prove the legal rights to the property, the ownership was contested, and eventually an association of Parisian restaurant and café owners gained control. Many years later our lady from Bourgogne stood by the bedside of her dying Grandmother and promised to fight as long and as hard as it would take to regain their family's rights to this property. A young lady in her 20's in 1959 when she began her courtroom crusade, it was in 2006, nearly 47 years later when the courts ruled in her favor and declared her the rightful owner. We can have only admiration and respect for the courageous determination and perseverance of this dear lady. Now in her 70's, and weary from years of legal battles she no longer felt she could administrate such an imposing piece of property, so she put it up for sale, with a price tag of 60 to 80 million euros, (between 75 and 100 million dollars). A treasure indeed for her and her family. But did this treasure arrive too late to do her much good? Seeking only peace and quiet for her latter years she will have the satisfaction of having won this great battle, and her family will never have need of want, but at her age the treasure will have little to offer. Gone are the years of youth and strength when this fortune could have opened the doors to the world, through travel and learning. Gone are the years of youthful initiative when such a fortune could have been the foundation for even greater accomplishments. It arrived in her life much like a beautiful bouquet of flowers on the table, after the departure of the lady for whom they were intended.

Many people spend their whole lives chasing treasures that arrive too late, or not at all. But there is a treasure that will never arrive too late if we seek it. It is faith and trust in the Lord Jesus Christ! The Bible warns us: *"Lay not up for yourselves treasures upon earth, where moth and rust doth corrupt, and where thieves break through and steal: But lay up for yourselves treasures in Heaven, where neither moth nor rust doth corrupt, and where thieves do not break through nor steal: For where your treasure is, there will your heart be also." (Matthew 6: 19-21)* Faith and salvation in the Lord Jesus Christ is a treasure you can have today, and you can keep it for life and eternity!

ARE YOU HAPPY?

W ell? What about it? Are you happy? If not, what would it take to make you happy? Most public surveys asking that same question would undoubtedly reveal the same answer for most people, even in our modern, industrialized world. Money! More wealth! Most people still feel that having more money would make them happier, even though we currently live in an age when the average worker has a higher salary than ever before, and he is working fewer hours to obtain it. Other benefits and attributions make our current generation the most comfortable one to have ever existed. Yet, our modern homes, our futuristic automobiles, fashionable clothes, and sumptuous foods have not made us happier. So the question is not out of place: "Are you happy?"

Proverbs 14:13 is an interesting verse on this subject, as we read: *"Even in laughter the heart is sorrowful; and the end of that mirth is heaviness."* We have all laughed when we did not feel like it, trying to mask the hurt within our hearts. Laughter does not necessarily mean one is happy. Many have been the comedians, comics or clowns that have spent their lives making others laugh, while they themselves led dreary, miserable, unhappy existences. Many of them had money, but that did not bring happiness. Neither did fame, nor power, nor influence.

Another case in point would be the French General and President of the French Republic, General Charles de Gaulle. Notice this conversation that took place between the General and Emmanuel d'Astier, a highly respected journalist and political figure in the days following World War Two. After completing his interview with the General, d'Astier spoke to de Gaulle in a warm and concerned way as he asked point blank:

—Mon General! Etes-vous heureux? ("My General, are you happy?")

The startled President responded with this stern and bitter reply:

—D'Astier, vous perdez la tete!...Vous savez bien que le bonheur n'existe pas.

("D'Astier, you have lost your head! You know very well that happiness doesn't exist!")

De Gaulle had everything most men could ask for: wealth, power, influence, and so much more. Yet, according to his own words he was not happy. You may find yourself in a similar situation, of having succeeded in nearly everything in life, except in the realm of happiness. There is an answer for that need. The Bible tells us in Isaiah 65:14: *"Behold, my servants shall sing for joy of heart, but ye shall cry for sorrow of heart, and shall howl for vexation of spirit."*

In this verse of Scripture we see both sides of the question. Some shall sing for joy, while others shall cry for sorrow of heart. The key to the promise of this verse is in the words, "my servants". Being a servant of the Most High will bring joy. To not be His servant can only bring sorrow. The path to true happiness takes you by way of the cross of Jesus Christ, through salvation by faith in Him. That same path will also take you to complete surrender to God and His will for your life. Rebellion to the will of God will destroy any hope of happiness. Why are so many people unhappy, in spite of their worldly possessions? Because they have not come to Christ in salvation and submission, the only true path to happiness, joy, and satisfaction in life. Step out on that pathway today. Just as there is room at the cross for you, there is also room for you on the pathway to a happy and fulfilled life in Christ!

CONSIDER THE END OF THEIR CONVERSATION: PART ONE

Through the centuries there have been many people who have tried to cause the public to follow them, leading them about much like a bull with a ring in its nose. Some have been politicians; others were writers, philosophers, military leaders, or revolutionaries. There are many people like that today. The Bible warns us about whom we choose to follow. Hebrews 13:7 tells us: *"Remember them which have the rule over you, who have spoken unto you the Word of God: whose faith follow, considering the end of their conversation."*

This passage is speaking about the good people God has sent along in our lives to help us. We are to consider, or look at the way they come to the end of their lives, and follow the faith we see in them. There are four words in the Greek that express the end of something, such as the end of a job, or a limit or boundary. The word translated "end" here in Hebrews 13:7 is the word, "ekbasis" and it means, "a way out; an issue". God is telling us here to look at the whole lives of our spiritual leaders, and then consider their faith as death draws near to them.

But what kind of an end have these so called leaders of mankind produced? Would we care to follow them to a similar deathbed such as they found for themselves as their lives came to a close? Let us take time to listen to what some of them had to say as they approached the end of their lives, and the shadow of the specter of death fell coldly across their faces. Consider their end.

Napoleon: "I am dying before my time, and my body will be returned to the earth as food for worms. So is the destiny of the one they called 'The Great Napoleon'.

What a great abyss exists between my profound misery and the eternal kingdom of Christ!"

Mirabeau, (A great public speaker during the French revolution): "Give me some more laudanum, (an opium based medication), so that I will not be able to think about eternity!"

Queen of England, Elizabeth I, (1533-1603). Under her reign England became a world power, and she became immensely wealthy. Her fabulous gowns dripped with jewelry, and yet as she lay dying she could only cry out in desperation: "All of my possessions for a moment of time!"

Pablo Picasso died in 1973 at the age of 91. With family and friends gathered about him and knowing the end was near, what would be the last words of the world renowned artist? Would he seek spiritual help to be prepared to meet the God he had so often scoffed at? Would he seek a copy of Scriptures, or ask for prayer? With some of his last breaths taken here on earth the prolific artist could think of nothing better to say than: "Drink to me!"

British novelist D. H. Lawrence was best known for his sexually explicit novel, Lady Chatterley's Lover. His own life was similar to his novels, with few interdictions. In 1930, at the age of just 44, he found himself wasted away to a mere 85 pounds as he cried out in delirium upon his deathbed. Near the end he called out for his friend, Maria Christina Chambers, pleading: "Maria, don't let me die!" Of course she could do nothing to avoid the unavoidable, as Lawrence went into eternity to meet the God he had never wished to acknowledge. Where a person has been is not near as important as where he is going. Some have sat in power, wealth, and fame, before having lost it all and finishing in poverty and misery. Before following someone, let us consider where their trail will lead us!

CONSIDER THE END OF THEIR CONVERSATION: PART TWO

In our preceding study we sought to understand the importance of Hebrews 13:7 where we are told to watch closely our spiritual leaders in life: *"Whose faith follow, considering the end of their conversation."* Knowing that many people do not wish to heed this Scriptural injunction, preferring instead to follow misguided and misguiding leaders of the world, we took note of the sad way in which so many of them ended their lives. It would however, be a great injustice to the grace of God if we were to look only at those sad examples, for God's children throughout the ages have shown us the way when it comes to stepping across the threshold from life into eternity. Consider the end of these conversations!

John Huss was a powerful preacher of the Gospel in the early 1400's, coming to Christ thanks to the writings of John Wycliffe. His preaching so bothered the church of Rome that a plan was put in place to dispose of him. He was betrayed, imprisoned without due trial, and condemned to be burned at the stake. As the flames encompassed his body, his lungs scorched by the intense heat, John Huss drew his last breaths here on earth to sing the hymn: "Jesus Christ, the Son of the living God, have mercy on me!" He led the way in noble courage.

The name of David Livingstone will always be one of the first to come to mind when we think of the great men of God that have gone before us, showing us the way in Christian service. This great Scottish missionary first thought to go as a missionary to China, but when the Opium War in China closed that door he turned to Africa, bringing the Light of the Gospel to the Dark Continent for 30 years until his death. Covering one-third of the African continent in his travels he faced many hardships. He was attacked and severely maimed by a lion, he was often in danger from warring tribes and slave traders of whom he was a resounding adversary, and his body was constantly wracked with pain and fever from jungle illnesses. No words could describe his immense pain as he dug a shallow grave there in the heart of the jungle to bury his beloved wife. Throwing himself prostate upon the fresh mound of earth he cried out: "Oh my Mary, my Mary! I loved you when I married you, and the longer I lived with you, I loved you the more!" Standing back from her grave under a large baobab tree, he said simply: "For the first time in my life I feel willing to die!"

Yet, after a time of mourning Livingstone raised his eyes to the jungle pathway leading deeper into the interior, summoned the small group of converts traveling with him, and pushed on. Deeper and deeper he pushed into the jungle, taking the Gospel to village after village, until he had used up every ounce of strength and health left within him. Eleven years after burying his precious wife, Livingstone was nearing his end. A hastily built hut was put up quickly for him; his fever wracked body was laid on a cot. His native friends stood watch throughout the night as best as they could, but after a while all was quiet in the hut. In the cold grey light of the dawn Livingstone was found dead, not in his bed, but beside it, in a position of prayer! He had spent his last moments on earth communing with the Saviour he had so faithfully served; the One who met with him there to usher him from that makeshift hut, into the heavenlies!

May we take heed to Psalm 37: 35-37, *"I have seen the wicked in great power, and spreading himself like a green bay tree. Yet he passed away, and, lo, he was not: yea, I sought him, be he could not be found. Mark the perfect man, and behold the upright: for the end of that man is peace!"*

THE INESCAPABILITY
OF DEATH

The story is so strange that it defies belief. One cannot be blamed for being skeptical about these events, though it is said that there is a stone monument on the island of Sicily marking the death of the man in question. His name was Aeschylus, (525-456 BC), a Greek dramatist known to have written about 90 plays. Born in Eleusis near Athens, he began early to write tragic poetry and with time was considered the father of Greek tragedy. Only about 7 of his works are still known to exist today.

During his youth Aeschylus was part of the Grecian army, fighting against the Persians at Marathon in 490 BC, and at Salamis in 480 BC. He served his country well, escaped many dangers, and eventually returned to private life taking up once again his neglected quill and parchments. His tragedies were highly acclaimed, his wealth and public stature growing accordingly.

Yet, a dark cloud came into his life. Aeschylus allowed a fortune teller to convince him that death would come to him from the sky in a most unusual manner. Danger was imminent! He must be wary! Taking the misguided medium seriously Aeschylus became afraid to venture out of doors, except on rare occasions. On a stormy day he would shelter himself in the innermost recesses of his home, afraid a bolt of lightning would be the fulfillment of the fortune teller's oracle. His thirst for travel and learning were too strong for him to remain at home forever, so he often made fearful trips to places of attraction. During his lifetime he made his way three times to the Italian island of Sicily. It was during his third such visit that he lost his life while visiting the town of Gela. He had looked first to the skies before venturing out, but the sky was an immaculate blue, without a cloud in sight. Feeling safe he stopped to rest as he contemplated the beauty of this volcanic isle. Suddenly, a great weight dropped from the sky, hitting him squarely on the head, killing him instantly. An eagle had taken a large turtle in its claws and following his instincts he flew high in the sky until he found an appropriate rock below on which to drop his prey, breaking it open and allowing him to enjoy his feast. From his vantage point in the sky the bald, shining head of Aeschylus must have seemed to him like just such a rock. His aim was true, the shell of the turtle was deadly, and Aeschylus came to his untimely and strange end. The town of Gela erected a stone monument to him there.

The ancient Greek poet misunderstood the same thing as so many people today. The greatest question of life is not to know how you will die, nor where you will die. Knowing when you will die is not the greatest question of all either. Most important, you need to know if you are ready to die! As someone has said: "If you are not ready to die, you are not ready to live!" How true that is! The Bible reminds us: *"What man is he that liveth, and shall not see death? Shall he deliver his soul from the hand of the grave?"* *(Psalm 89:48)* We must not fool ourselves, the question is not, "How?" or "Where?" or even "When?" but rather, "Am I ready for death at any time, any place?

It is a shame that Aeschylus did not manage to put his trust in the Scriptures instead of a soothsayer.

What comfort Psalm 48:14 could have been to him: *"For this God is our God for ever and ever: He will be our guide even unto death"*. May your trust be in the only true and living God, and in His Holy Word! Faith in Him will give you peace for your life, and assurance for all eternity!

THIS POOR MAN CRIED

Though I do like good documentation, I have had great difficulty in researching this story. In spite of my best efforts I have only found this story recorded one time, though it was by a reputable source. I could not help but see myself in this authentic story of Etienne Laine, (1747-1822), a street vendor of vegetables in the heart of Paris. Selling whatever was in season he would go from street to street with his wares on his back, selling them as he went, knowing that the livelihood of his family depended on him returning home that evening with his backpack empty, and his few coins of profit in his pocket. Even in the best of days it was barely enough to survive on, as the 27 year old fellow saw more misery than money, and little hope for the future.

However, little did Laine know that things were about to change on this particular day in 1774, as he gathered his wares together and set out as usual for the narrow, winding streets of Paris. Today he would be selling a seasonal favorite, asparagus. He always did well with that when it was in season. His booming voice, strong from years of plying his trade in this manner, could easily be heard as he called out: "Buy my asparagus! Buy my asparagus!" Etienne, (Stephen, in English) soon found himself working one of his favorite areas, around the majestic Paris Opera House where he knew the owners of the chic shops and well to do residents could more easily afford his delicacies than the average Parisian. Working his way down a narrow side street beside the Opera his voice resounded off the stone walls of the "House of Molière" and the building beside it, being even more amplified than usual. Just above the clamor and din of the streets was the office of the Director for the Paris Opera House. His attention was drawn away from his work as his ears picked up the voice of Etienne Laine passing under his window in the street below. Leaning back in his chair he was enthralled by that voice. What power! What force! He could hardly believe his ears! Suddenly, a window cracked and broke under the power of the street vendor's voice. The Director sprang from his chair, rushed to the window and beckoned for Laine to come immediately to his office. An assistant was sent down to direct the young man to the Director's office, and Etienne Laine's life would never again be the same.

Etienne Laine went on to become one of the greatest operatic singers of his generation. Fame and fortune were his. Security was provided for him and his family, thanks to one man that saw something in young Etienne that no one else seemed to notice. His magnificent voice was finally put to good use, under the watchful care of his new found friend.

I was so much like that! There was a time when I wandered the meandering side streets of life, just trying to get by as best as I knew how. But all of my efforts could not take away my lost, sinful condition, and the continual spiritual misery in which I found myself. Then one day, "Someone" from above heard my woeful cry, called me unto Himself, saved my miserable soul, and gave me something to live for. God heard my cry and saw in me something that no one else seemed to see, He drew me unto Himself, and my life has never again been the same.

If I said I could see myself in this story of Etienne Laine, I can see myself even more in Psalm 34:6, *"This poor man cried, and the Lord heard him, and saved him out of all his troubles."* Dear reader friend, should you still be wandering in the hopelessness of your lost condition, call out unto the only true God of heaven, who will hear you, and is able to save you out of all your troubles!

"WHO WILL PAY MY DEBT?"

The room was dark and foreboding. Few would have imagined it to be the room of one of Napoleon's finest young officers. An oil lamp setting on the table against the back wall of the room did its best to enlighten the night with its silvery glow. Before the table sat Napoleon's young officer, a young man with a promising career under the Emperor, having come from a wealthy and influential family. But the dancing light of the lamp could bring no cheer to the young officer, for he had been bitten by the demon of gambling, and by the turn of the card and the roll of the dice he had squandered his entire fortune. Now, in a time of desperation he has decided to end his life. Carefully taking his pistol from his belt, checking it to be sure it was ready to fire, he lays it before him on the table. Before taking his life he wants to leave a last, written farewell to his parents.

He wrote: "I was young and rich. I had a brilliant career before me, but I have ruined my life. I have played, and I have lost everything; my fortune and my honor. I am crushed by a huge debt. But who will pay my debt?" Fatigue and a weary spirit caused the young man to lay aside his quill pen, lay his head beside the tragic sheet of white paper, and fall into a deep sleep.

A short while later Napoleon came looking for the young officer, who had missed an appointment with him. Tapping gently on the door and receiving no reply, he pushed the door quietly open and saw the young man asleep at his desk. Stepping softly closer he saw the pistol and the note. Understanding the gravity of the situation, and moved by profound sympathy for the young man, he took the quill pen in hand, dipped it quickly into the ink pot at the head of the table, and beside the seemingly hopeless question of the young officer, with large and firm letters he wrote: "I, THE EMPEROR!" One can only imagine the joy and relief of the young officer when he awakened and found that it was the Emperor himself who had promised to pay his debt, and relieve him of his fears.

This is what Paul told Philemon when, concerning the possible debts of the runaway slave Onesimus, he said: *"If he hath wronged thee, or oweth thee ought, put that on mine account." (Philemon 18)* Paul used the word "if" to speak of Onesimus' possible debts. We should have no such doubt, for our sin debt before God is great, and as Napoleon's young officer, we can see no way out on our own, needing someone to pay our debt for us. If not, our lives too would come to a tragic end in a dark and lonely room of desperation.

There was a time when my sins brought me to a place of hopeless despair as I too asked the question: "Who will pay my debt?" I asked the question, but no man stepped forward to volunteer. My heart trembled as I thought of the prospects of facing eternity with this debt still on my account. Then came Jesus, stepping forward and taking my sins upon Himself on the cross. Like this young soldier, I awakened from my stupor to find this promise written before me: *"But He was wounded for our transgressions, He was bruised for our iniquities: the chastisement of our peace was upon Him, and with His stripes we are healed." (Isaiah 53:5)* Napoleon paid from his purse, but Jesus paid in His person. Napoleon acted out of pity, but Jesus acted out of love. Napoleon had pity on one of his officers, but, *"God so loved the **world** that He gave"*... Dear reader, are you still burdened by a debt of sin? If so, then come by faith to Christ who has paid that debt, and allow Him to apply that debt to His account!

CALL HIM "MR. PUGNACIOUS"

The photo of the elderly couple in the newspaper caught my attention. A special ceremony was being held for them in the retirement home where they reside on the North-West coast of France. Andre and Raymonde were joined in marriage November 29, 1930 in the Northern town of Lille, (Raymonde, spelled with an "e" at the end of it, is the feminine form of Raymond, as is the case of many first names in French). Born in 1908 they had lived through both World Wars. But now today is their 75th wedding anniversary; their alabaster anniversary. Alabaster, how fitting! It is a fine grained gypsum, snow white, translucent, and has been a favorite of craftsmen since ancient times. This makes it even more interesting when we see Jesus at Bethany in the house of Simon the leper and Mary of Bethany comes with: *"an alabaster box of very precious ointment"* and anoints the head of the Saviour as He sat at meat, (Matthew 26:7). Only a person of means could have had an alabaster box, and only the most precious of things would have been kept within. Just as it was for Andre and Raymonde, who kept the precious union of their lives within the alabaster box of their sacred marriage vows.

The newspaper article also drew my attention to the fighting spirit shown by Andre during World War Two. Drafted into the French Navy, Andre found himself trapped and neutralized with French forces at Lorient. Being a "Resistant" by heart he escaped and by bicycle he made the long journey back to Lille, narrowly avoiding the many German patrols and barricades. Eventually captured he was sent to Germany to work as a forced laborer, where he somehow found a way to sabotage a German tank, bringing the ire of the German authorities upon him, who sent him to one of their infamous concentration camps, from which few walked away. But walk away he did, for the tenacious spirit of Andre was undaunted, and once again he somehow managed to escape. Making his way by foot Andre often moved at night, hid and slept by day, until he once again trod on the familiar sod of Northern France. Rejoining the French Resistance he was constantly engaged in sabotage and hit and run tactics until the victory was won, liberation had come, and he and Raymonde could pick up the thread of their long lives together. Many wonderful superlatives could be used to describe this exemplary patriot. I say, call him: "Mr. Pugnacious" in the most honorable sense. Pugnacious is someone that is combative, bellicose, or having a fighting spirit. Andre certainly was that, and how much he has been an honor to his country for it.

The apostle Paul had that same fighting spirit, as we see in II Timothy 4:7-8, where Paul says: *"I have fought a good fight, I have finished my course, I have kept the faith: Henceforth there is laid up for me a crown of righteousness, which the Lord, the righteous Judge, shall give me at that day: and not to me only, but unto all them also that love His appearing."* We also see this in the book of Hebrews chapter 11 where God mentions the names of such valiant servants as Gedeon, Barak, Samson, Jephthae, David, Samuel and the prophets, who stood their ground for God, and: *"waxed valiant in fight" (verse 34).*

God is looking for some pugnacious people today, in this same way. Christians who will stand for God and His Word, and will continue the combat for the truth until Christ comes again and the final victory is won. Have you weakened in battle Christian friend? Then take heart and resolve as Paul to finish your course and faithfully run the race that God has set before you!

THE SCHOOLGIRL
AND THE KING

This little Prussian town was in total, absolute effervescence. Never before had this small Germanic village experienced anything quite like it, for their King was coming to pay them a visit! The mayor was beside himself. Would everything be ready and appropriate for the King? Litter was cleaned from the streets; every home was made as appealing as possible for the passing royal cortege. But most of all the school must be made ready, for had not the King said he wished to stop there, meet the school master and speak to the children? The village people would remember this day forever!

The monumental day finally arrived and the royal procession slowly made its way into town. After speaking with the mayor and greeting the town's people the King made his way to the school where he was warmly welcomed by one and all, and a speech was given. As the children looked on the King then stepped forward and taking an orange from a plate he turned to the young students and tested them by asking: "To what kingdom does this belong?"

The children could only look timidly at one another; none of them had ever spoken to a King before. Finally one young girl spoke up and said: "The vegetable kingdom, Sire". Pleased with the correct answer the King slipped his hand into his vest pocket and brought forth a gold coin. "And to what kingdom does this belong?" he asked. Feeling more confident now the same little girl responded: "To the mineral kingdom, Sire". A smile of pleasure on his face, the King looked squarely at the tassel headed young waif before him and proceeded by asking: "And to what kingdom do I belong then?" This question troubled the girl greatly, for she did not wish to say, "The animal kingdom" though she knew that was the expected answer. For this was the King, and she could not bring herself to compare her King to an animal! Her tiny heart trembled and her mind raced frantically to think of how to respond.

And then she remembered some of the Bible lessons she had learned, how that "God made man in His own image," so looking up she replied: "To God's kingdom, Sire!" The King was speechless. A deep look of compassion came across his face and those standing near swore that they saw tears form in his eyes. Placing his hand gently on the child's head he said with emotion: "God grant that I may be accounted worthy of that kingdom!" The heart felt words of a little child had moved the heart of a King.

To which kingdom do you belong? There are only two you know: either the kingdom of God, or the kingdom of Satan. It is the kingdom of light as compared to the kingdom of darkness; the kingdom of hope or the kingdom of despair. There is only one way to enter the heavenly kingdom as we see in Colossians 1:13-14 where Paul speaks of God: *"Who hath delivered us from the power of darkness, and hath translated us into the kingdom of His dear Son: In whom we have redemption through His blood, even the forgiveness of sins."* Have you entered that kingdom by faith in the redemptive work of Christ? If not, may the words of that little girl speak to your heart as they did to the heart of her King!

THE HUNGARIAN FARMER'S UNKNOWN FORTUNE

Our story begins in Chicago in the early 1900's, where we find the highly skilled and widely recognized cutter of precious stones, Gustaf Gillman, working quietly in his exquisite little shop. The noise of the front door softly opening alerts Mr. Gillman's attention, as he lifts his head to greet the customer, a rugged, simple man, seemingly from the country. "Hello, my name is John Mihok, and I was wondering if you could cut and polish this stone?" he said, as he slowly unfolded the fabric surrounding a large, red stone taken from his pocket. Gustaf Gillman stepped back in shock and awe as this unexpected spectacle burst upon his sight, for there on the counter before him was the largest pigeon-red ruby he had ever seen in his life, and he had seen many. Could it be for real? After several minutes of extreme scrutiny the verdict was pronounced, this huge ruby was authentic, and nearly perfect in every way!

Mihok explained that the stone had always belonged to his family ever since the day when his father, Michel Mihok found it while plowing their fields back home in their native Hungary. His father often turned over many stones with his horse drawn plow, but the beautiful color of this one caught his attention causing him to take it home, leaving it in a drawer. When John Mihok immigrated to America in 1903 the stone was tossed into the bottom of a suitcase. Over the years since then his children played with it, and some even cut their teeth on it, but never did he think it of any value. How quick Mr. Gillman was to point out that error!

Pigeon-red rubies are the most sought after of all rubies, and this one was perfect. When masterfully cut into a magnificent ruby it weighed 23 and 9/10 carats, with a value estimated at well over a quarter of a million dollars, though its value would far transcend that figure in the years to come. This veritable fortune had gone unnoticed by these humble farmers for well over half a century.

How terrible it is that mankind is so often like that in regards to the Lord Jesus Christ, for the Lord Jesus is a veritable treasure, so often unnoticed by those that pass so closely by. This ruby was trampled under foot for many years until the plow turned it up to full view, and even then it was left languishing in a drawer or a suitcase for another generation. Does not the Scriptures remind us that: *"Again, the kingdom of heaven is like unto treasure hid in a field; the which when a man hath found, he hideth, and for joy thereof goeth and selleth all that he hath, and buyeth that field."* *(Matthew 13:44)* Jesus Christ is certainly a: "Great Treasure" and any man of good sense and a clear mind will want to do all he can to possess that magnificent "Treasure" for himself. What we need today is not a pigeon-red ruby, but the precious red blood: *"of the Lamb slain from the foundation of the world."* *(Revelation 13:8)* This treasure is not obtained by work nor by purchase, but by a child-like faith placed in the finished work of the Lord Jesus Christ on the cross of Calvary. Don't neglect it..... accept Him!

THE STUPID PLOUGHBOY

Very few people placed much faith in the mental abilities of poor John Hunt, a simple minded ploughboy who could more often be seen setting on a fence staring blankly into space, than working the fields given to his charge. Local farmers were reluctant to employ the "stupid ploughboy" for even the simplest errands. Little hope was given for his future, that is, until the day young John Hunt found Christ as Saviour, and his life was changed. When the love of God touched his heart a dormant intellect was aroused along with a zeal for the things of God. He quickly learned to read and write, with time he began to preach, and was eventually recommended as a candidate for the ministry.

The time came for John Hunt to go to London for his examination into the ministry. Yet his "stupid ploughboy" image and reputation followed him there and he saw his demand for entrance into the school of theology refused. Every member of the council voted that he be sent home again, except for one man, Dr. Hannah, who begged for Hunt to be taken into theological training on a trial basis. "I believe there is something in him" he said. And so thus began the precarious theological training of the young man from the farmlands.

Seizing his chance to prove himself John Hunt worked hard to correct his deplorable country accent; he studied the Greek New Testament on his knees in prayer and tears, and succeeded. He preached with amazing zeal and power, and began to master the basics of linguistics. Leaving for the Fiji Islands as a missionary Hunt began to reduce the barbarous language of those islands into a grammatical form, opening up the reading of the Bible to them, and eventually seeing literally thousands of these islanders turn from their former darkness to the light of the Gospel of Christ. Years later, when facing death, John Hunt was heard to say: "Oh that I could run up to the top of Vewa Hill, and fill the whole island with a shout of glory!"

What turned this "stupid ploughboy" into such a successful missionary? The answer is rather simple. John Hunt knew how to couple his zeal with old fashioned hard work! Aware of his mental weaknesses the former farmer decided to apply himself in working hard at making something of himself for God. And work hard, he did! Does not the Bible tell us that the Lord Jesus shall come again:..."*and then He shall reward every man according to his works.*" *(Matthew 16:27)* According to his works, He said. Not according to our intellect, not according to the diplomas we may have attained, not according to our bank account, nor our musical talent, but according to our works. *"Work out your own salvation with fear and trembling"* Paul told the Philippians, (2:12). May we roll up our sleeves and get to work, because hard work, still.....works!

ON LOSING YOUR LIFE
IN CHRIST

There are some passages of Scripture that are rather easy for the mind to understand and retain, but the heart may find them somewhat difficult to put into practice. Passages dealing with, for example, the importance of prayer, faithfulness to the house of God, on tithing and giving, or the need to be a faithful witness. In Matthew 10: 37-39 Jesus is giving instructions to His 12 disciples before sending them out, when He gives them an order that we can all understand, but may have difficulty in implementing. Here is what He said: *"He that loveth father or mother more than me is not worthy of me: and he that loveth son or daughter more than me is not worthy of me. And he that taketh not his cross,*

and followeth after me, is not worthy of me. He that findeth his life shall lose it: and he that loseth his life for my sake shall find it."

Does this mean that we are no longer to hold any natural affection for our own flesh and blood? Absolutely not! But God does expect His children to be able to offer Him a love and devotion that is far greater than anything man can offer family and friends. And the closer we get to this devotion to God, the more we will be able to love our loved ones in a greater and better way.

Perhaps the great Scottish missionary John G. Paton can help us understand better this passage of Scripture. John Gibson Paton, (1824-1907) was born near Dumfries, Scotland to humble Christian parents, being one of 5 sons and 6 daughters. John grew up seeing his father pray 3 times a day for the needs of the family. Living for others was a part of their family life. At the age of 12 John was studying Latin and Greek, before leaving for Glasgow to study medicine and theology. He began a ministry to the poor in the slums of Glasgow, and in the following 10 years saw many of them won to Christ, with a number of them going into the ministry. Then came a call for missionaries to go to the New Hebrides Islands of the South

Pacific, long known for their cannibalistic inhabitants. This call touched the heart of Paton, and he was determined to try and reach these pagan people for Christ. Many of his friends tried to convince Paton that he was needed much more there where he was, and that sacrificing his life in this way profited little. Even his professor and pastor, Dr. Symington, tried to dissuade him from leaving. The pressure was great upon him. What would he do?

One dear old Christian friend came often at Paton with the same argument: "The cannibals! You will be eaten by the cannibals!" Paton's reply shows his true understanding and acceptance of Christ's words in Matthew 10, when he said:

"Mr. Dickson, you are advanced in years now, and your own prospect is soon to be laid in the grave, there to be eaten by worms; I confess to you that if I can live and die, serving and honoring the Lord Jesus, it will make no difference to me whether I am eaten by cannibals, or by worms; and in the Great Day my resurrection body will rise as fair as yours in the likeness of our risen Redeemer!"

Perhaps those words of John Paton will help us see that losing our life in Christ means that we let God set the limits as to what we do, where we go, and under what circumstances. Our life is no longer our own, and we make no claim to it, in spite of possible protests of family and friends. If our life is "lost" in Christ it may seem truly lost to others, but we may rest assured that God knows where it is; in His care and providence. And he that plants his life in Christ, much like a seed in the fallow ground of God's service, will live to see the fruit it bears in eternity's dawning light!

THE PRINCE'S
GREAT SHAME

How can one tell the worth of a man? By what rule of measurement can one's character be esteemed noble or ignoble? That is the question we will face today as we look at the life and work of the Prussian Prince Frederick Charles, or, "Friedrich Carl", (1828-1885). Born in Berlin as the only son of Prince Carl, a brother of the powerful Prussian Emperor William I, King of Prussia from 1861 until 1888. William I sought Prussian expansion, accomplished with the help of Prime Minister, Otto von Bismarck, who completely reformed the Prussian army, leading them to victories over Denmark in 1864, at Sadowa in 1866, and over France in 1871.

Young Prince Charles was more than happy to enter into the Prussian army under his Uncle, William I. Military life pleased him, as he moved quickly to the rank of General, showing a remarkable grasp of military science and strategy. In the Danish war of 1849 he proved himself brave and brilliant as he was accredited with having solely developed the strategy for the deciding win at Schleswig. His name was on every tongue in Prussia, because of his cunning and brilliance. But Prince Charles had one major flaw in his character, which the public had not yet seen.

Shortly after his successful siege of Duppel in February 1864, Prince Charles came into full command of the Prussian army as field marshal, beginning a long series of remarkable victories. He led the victory over the Austrian armies at Sadowa in 1866. Again, it was on his military brilliance that Prime Minister Bismarck counted as the Prussians defeated the French in 1871, which eventually allowed William I to be proclaimed Emperor in the famous "Hall of Mirrors" at the Palace of Versailles, just outside of Paris. Though Prince Charles's role in this was huge, that fatal flaw in his character was about to bring about his downfall.

Prince Charles was a brilliant tactician on the battlefield, but a miserable tyrant in his own home. He openly neglected his dear wife and children, leaving them in extreme poverty. His conduct when home was unbearable, his wife being reduced to little better than a slave, and the simplest soldier in his army fared none the worse than his own children at home. Calls were made to the Emperor himself to do something about the impoverished condition of this family. The Emperor could not turn a blind eye to the brutal despotism of his nephew. Prince Charles was forced into retirement to a family home in the rural district near Potsdam, where the once brilliant military strategist spent his last days in disgrace and solitude, until his death in 1885, forgotten by most, and mourned by few. The greatness of his military career could not mask the poorness of his personal character.

It has been said that a man is no better a man than he is at home. The conduct of a man before his wife and children is the true test of a man's quality. It means little to be applauded in public if one is despised and feared at home. Many men have received awards and accolades for their work done on the silver screen, on the stage, in music, or in politics, while having been total failures as husbands and fathers, which adds nothing to their stature as a man. Does not the Bible remind us: "But if any provide not for his own, and specially for those of his own house, he has denied the faith, and is worse than an infidel." (I Timothy 5:8) Or again: *"Likewise, ye husbands, dwell with them according to knowledge, giving honour unto the wife, as unto the weaker vessel, and as being heirs together of the grace of life; that your prayers be not hindered." (I Peter 3:7) A truly great man is one that has merited the love and respect of his wife, and has proven himself a worthy example for his children to follow, in the paths of the Lord!*

THE DEATH OF A DOVE

My wife never ceases to amaze me. During our years of ministry in France we rarely had much of a back yard, but my dear wife was always able to coax a remarkable number of birds into that tiny space. The little chickadees, finches and various warblers welcomed her grain feeder, bread crumbs, and the grease balls in the winter. Their merry singing outside our kitchen window was a balm to our hearts as they sang the songs God gave them. We were especially pleased to receive regular visits from two couples of doves, whose presence seemed to bring a certain peace and serenity to our tiny patch of green. The blackbirds that sometimes alighted in our yard would chase the other birds away, confiscating all yardly possessions for their lone benefit. Not so the doves, this world renowned image of peace. The smaller birds of our feathered congregation knew this fact as the chickadees and doves pecked away, side by side, the little ones lost in song, the doves cooing softly along side them.

Looking through our kitchen window one day I noticed one of the doves laying much too quietly under the low limbs of a small fir tree. Approaching her quietly our fears were confirmed as we found her lifeless. We dug a deep hole towards the back of our garden, wrapped the lady dove in a clean cloth and laid her to rest. Knowing that doves are said to mate for life we wondered what her mate would do when he returned. We didn't have long to wait as he later flew in and seemed to be searching for her. He eventually sat down under a small shrub, withdrew into a crimped position and seldom moved. From time to time he ventured forth, inspecting the various corners of the garden where he and his mate would usually go, only to return alone to that little shrub and his inanimate position. This went on like this until the other couple of doves returned. They went straight to him, cooing fervently as they stood on each side of him, slowly drawing him back to life. I later saw him raise himself up and follow them to some of the fallen grain from my wife's feeder where he began to peck a few grains of seed. Within a day or two the three of them could be seen in flight or at rest, but almost always together. I had the distinct feeling that they had saved his life and had given him hope for living.

This reminds me of the place of the dove in Scriptures. There are between 350 and 400 different kinds of birds in Palestine, with at least 26 of them found nowhere else in the world. There are about 50 different kinds of birds mentioned in the Bible, with the dove holding a special place. The dove was the lowliest of the Old Testament sacrifices, being acceptable to the poorest of families. In the New Testament we see: *"...the Spirit of God descending like a dove,"* upon the Lord Jesus at the time of His baptism, (Matthew 3:16). The dove has long been a symbol of love, peace and meekness. Did we say, "meekness"?

Matthew 5:5 tells us: *"Blessed are the meek: for they shall inherit the earth."* The meek shall inherit the earth? Is that possible? Conquest is meant for the strong, is it not? Yet, meekness is stronger than muscle or steel. Meekness overcomes, while strength eventually fades away. Napoleon thought strength was the only way, but he found out otherwise as he died in isolated loneliness on Saint Helena. Hitler thought strength was the only way, until he came to a flaming suicidal end in his Berlin bunker. I Peter 3:4 reminds us: *"the ornament of a meek and quiet spirit, which is in the sight of God of great price."* Rocks will crumble, steel will rust, and muscles will weaken, but meekness will be victorious. Our friends the doves, remind us again of this truth.

WHEN DARWIN FINALLY GOT IT RIGHT

Mention the name of Charles Darwin and the average Bible believing Christian is ready to fight. Charles Darwin, (1809-1882) is well known for his theory on the evolutionary beginnings of mankind. This "theory" is nothing more than that, an unproven, undocumented, and unfounded theory that goes against Scriptures and the creation of all existence by God in the six literal days of creation, as seen in the first pages of the Bible. Yes, Darwin got it all wrong on that issue. However, many of today's teachers and proponents of the evolutionary theory have taken the idea much farther than Darwin intended. Perhaps this true event in the life of Charles Darwin will help us to better understand that fact.

It was around 1831 that Darwin visited Tierra del Fuego and found that the native people living there were the most debased and primitive people he had ever encountered. They had no houses, but only makeshift branch wigwams that could be put up in an hour. Sleeping on the dirt floor, uncovered and cold, they slept piled together like shivering snakes. Mostly naked, never washed, and covered with the blood and debris of their hunted prey they presented a ghastly sight. In time of war they were cannibals. When starving in the cold of winter they would strangle and eat their aged women and save their dogs for the hunt, saying simply: "Doggies catch otters; women no"!

Darwin was so repulsed by the deprived state of these people that he said it was: "Utterly useless to send missionaries to such a set of savages as the Fuegians, probably the very lowest of the human race"!

Fortunately, missionaries did not accept the opinion of Charles Darwin, and soon some men, such as Captain Gardner and Thomas Bridges, found their way to minister to this spiritually bankrupt people. The power of the Gospel had its effect, the savages were tamed; a Christian village was established at

Ooshooia, with a Church, a school, and an orphanage. Many parts of the Bible were translated into their native Tabgan tongue, and Gospel songs could be heard throughout the emerald green mountains!

Darwin eventually heard of the transformation that the Gospel brought to this savage people, bringing them decency and civilization, as well as the Gospel message. Darwin finally got it right when he wrote this: "The success of the Tierra del Fuego mission is most wonderful, and shames me, as I always prophesied utter failure." Darwin not only believed this enough to put it in print, but he followed it up with annual financial gifts to the Fuegian Mission that the mission might have the means to continue their ministry in that faraway land, taking the Gospel to every mountain and valley, to every tribe and village. Back home in England in the latter years of his life, and having seen what the power of the Gospel can do to change any people, Darwin organized preaching services at his country estate, inviting Gospel preachers to come and bring Bible messages to all those he could assemble there for the occasion.

When Darwin finally got it right he came into agreement with Proverbs 14:34, *"Righteousness exalteth a nation: but sin is a reproach to any people."* Yes, righteousness alone will exalt and lift up a nation. Politicians can't do it. Nor can the educators, philosophers, socialites or industrialists, for the Gospel alone can transform hearts and lives. The Gospel will raise up and improve the most pagan of people, but you don't have to be as "savage" as those distant people of Tierra del Fuego to need reviving by the Gospel of Jesus Christ. Without Christ we are all lost and undone. Do you need to come to Christ, today?

DON'T EVEN THINK
ABOUT IT

I know a three year old girl that shows more wisdom than many adults, at least on some occasions. While going for a walk she enjoys sailing right through mud puddles, sending the murky waters flying. But stern warnings from her parents, with the threat: "Don't even think about it!" brought a stop to such escapades. On one occasion she saw she was approaching an inviting mud puddle, but as she skirted carefully around it she was heard saying to herself: "Don't even think about it!" What a shame that so many adults fail to show the same self restraint, as they attempt things that are not only foolish, but dangerous.

Take this Hungarian Countess for example. An avowed atheist she fought the things of God her whole life. Upon approaching death she gave orders that her tomb be sealed in a way that it could never again be opened. She ordered a plaque to be placed there giving her name and the date of her death, with this inscription: "Not to be opened for eternity!" She defied God to raise her from the dead. Unknownst to the cemetery workers, a simple acorn had fallen into the space around the Countess's coffin. With time that little acorn sprang to life and began to make its way to the surface of the ground. Bursting the tomb asunder this little acorn became a mighty oak tree, showing God's power to open any grave.

An atheist of Hanover, Germany had a similar idea. He too gave orders for his tomb to be sealed to prevent the resurrection of the dead. Iron bars were set in place to seal the tomb, with a two ton slab of granite set on top to cover it all. His inscription read: "This tomb has been sealed for eternity; it shall never be opened!" But once again God intervened. There in the dirt tossed into the bottom of the tomb was the seed of a poplar tree. By the force of nature this tiny seed began to grow and eventually broke those iron bars in two, pushed aside the two ton slab of granite, and opened the tomb for all eyes to see. It does not pay to defy God!

The French atheist Voltaire took great pleasure in attacking anything Christian. He said he would destroy Christianity in his lifetime, and see the Bible disappear completely. He died in 1778 in his Paris home, in the throes of unbelievable suffering and anguish as he faced the horrors of his self chosen fate. Almost exactly 100 years after his death his Paris home was purchased by a Bible Society, meaning that the Bible hater's home became a place where the Word of God was being sent out throughout Europe and around the world! It does not pay to defy God! Don't even think about it!

What tremendous words these are from Psalm 50:22, *"Now consider this, ye that forget God, lest I tear you in pieces, and there be none to deliver."* Nor does it pay to go against the Word of God. You cannot bring God's Word to naught, for He has promised: *"For verily I say unto you, Till heaven and earth pass, one jot or one tittle shall in no wise pass from the law, till all be fulfilled." (Matthew 5:18)*

Remember, when you oppose the Word of God you are opposing the God of the Word! Love God, and love His Word! Get to know Him through His

Holy Word, and seek to live for Him through the teaching of His Word, for He has loved you since before you were born. Above all, don't try to defy God or His Word. You don't have a chance. Don't even think about it!

WHY PARIS DIDN'T BURN

It is August, 1944 and it is the beginning of the end for Adolph Hitler and his dream of world conquest. The beaches of Normandy were stained with blood and strewn with debris as the D-Day Invasion began on June 6, 1944. Within two weeks the 175,000 original invasionary forces had swollen to more than 850,000 men as they moved towards Paris, often faster than their supply lines could keep up with them. The furious Fuhrer sent out this order: "Paris must not fall into the hands of the enemy, or else he must find it reduced to a field of ruins." Yes, Paris must burn!

To accomplish this somber task General Dietrich von Choltitz, commander of all of Paris, was given strict orders to burn Paris to the ground, to leave not one bridge standing, nor a single monument intact.

Choltitz hesitated. No less than nine times the Fuhrer repeated his commands, on one occasion asking: "Paris, is it burning?" Who was this man that dared defy Hitler himself? General Choltitz seemed a perfect choice for this task, having served his country with fervor in World War I, being wounded three times in doing so. Again in 1939 he led campaigns against Holland, Poland, Russia and Belgium, totally destroying Rotterdam and crushing Sebastopol under a deluge of thousands of cannon shells. But Choltitz had become disenchanted with the German leader. As he left a private meeting with Hitler shortly before taking command of Paris, Choltitz mumbled softly to a friend: "There is no doubt: I found myself setting face to face with a fool!"

Dietrich von Choltitz loved Paris. He loved her broad, tree lined boulevards with their sidewalk cafes and boutiques. He enjoyed crossing the same bridges and walking down the same cobble stone streets on which Napoleon strode.

So, on August 22 he dispatched the Swedish Consulate General, Raoul Nordling, to find the Allied Commander, General Dwight D. Eisenhower, asking him to hurry in the taking of Paris before it was forever too late. And hurry they did, as the lead group of the 2nd Armored Division entered Paris on August 24, and Paris was saved. On August 25 Choltitz was arrested at his headquarters at the Hotel Meurice, and at 3:30 pm he signed the rendition of Paris. In his 37 years of military career this was the first time he had refused to obey an order, but he just could not bring himself to the burning of Paris! When liberated at the end of the war Choltitz returned to his native Germany where he went into business. He died at Baden-Baden November 5, 1966, just 4 days short of his 72nd birthday.

"Paris, is it burning?" Hitler asked. "Not yet, we can answer, but it will one day, as will New York, London, Rome and all the rest!" For the Bible tells us: *"And I saw a new heaven and a new earth: for the first heaven and the first earth were passed away; and there was no more sea. And I John saw the holy city, new Jerusalem, coming down from God out of heaven, prepared as a bride adorned for her husband." (Revelation 21: 1-2)*

We can understand the love of someone for a certain city, but the Bible says that the day will come when they will all be destroyed and a new heaven and a new earth will be offered to the children of God. That is the city God's people needs to look for, as

Abraham did: *"For he, (Abraham), looked for a city which hath foundations, whose builder and maker is God." (Hebrews 11:10)* We may have to live with our feet in the dust of man made streets here below, but the child of God can live with his head and his heart fixed in the heavenlies, awaiting the place our Lord has prepared for us there!

DEATH OF AN ATHEIST

You would not have wanted to have been there. Not there in that house; not at that particular moment. Those that had to be there wished that they could have been elsewhere. The year is 1778, and the place is a simple but comfortable home on a narrow side street of Paris. The silence of the night is punctuated with chilling screams and groanings as had been the case for several days, as a renowned atheist lay on his deathbed. Even Paris, the "City of Lights" cannot drive the darkness away from this room as Francois Marie Arouet faces the horrors of a hopeless death. You would know this prolific writer by his pen name, Voltaire.

It started just a few nights before as Voltaire attended the representation of one of the plays he had written. The crowd acclaimed him and the play with such enthusiasm that he eventually stood and said: "Are you trying to kill me with pleasure?" These words were hardly pronounced when he was struck down with a violent hemorrhage. He was rushed to his home, the best Doctors were called in, and nurses were assigned to care for him night and day, to no avail. Day after day Voltaire slipped closer to death in the most horrible fashion. His physical sufferings were nothing compared to the agony felt in his soul and spirit. His physician, Dr. Tronchin, spoke often of the terrible mental anguish of his famous patient, as he faced his last hours. Ragings, blasphemies, cursings, invectives directed towards God, were all bathed in the sweat of desperation. Dr. Tronchin said the last hours of Voltaire were spent in total dementia. The nurse assigned to stay with him in his final hours swore to never again set at the deathbed of a dying atheist, it was too horrible!

The death of Voltaire, a life long adversary of anything Christian, brought no joy to God. To the contrary, the Bible says: *"Have I any pleasure at all that the wicked should die? saith the Lord God: and not that he should return from his ways, and live?"* *(Ezekiel 18:23)* Yes, God takes no pleasure in the death of even the worst of men, and He will take no pleasure in your death should you leave this life without Christ. What a difference it makes for those that have been saved by Christ, for the Bible says of them: *"Precious in the sight of the Lord is the death of His saints." (Psalm 116:15)* As Voltaire lay dying, sometimes agonizing on the floor, he said to Dr. Tronchin: "I am abandoned of God! Doctor, I will give you the half of all I possess if you would prolong my life by six months!" The Doctor replied: "Monsieur, you don't even have six weeks to live!" Voltaire never did understand that the price had already been paid, by the Lord Jesus-Christ he opposed so vehemently. Have you understood better than he?

Years before all this, Voltaire happened across a young boy reading his book of catechism in the shade of an apple tree. Hoping to destroy the lad's faith in God, he asked him: "Listen young man, I will give you all the apples of this orchard if you can tell me where God is!" The youngster raised his head slowly as he thought on the question, and respectfully said: "And you Sir, can you tell me where He is not?" Sadly, Voltaire has no doubt found that place where God is not. And the anguish of his deathbed could not be as great as the torments of a Christless eternity!

THE CROSS
BESIDE THE ROAD

As I read once again the newspaper article before me on my desk I find myself moved by human emotion as much as I was the first time I read it. The article speaks of the death of an 18 year old girl in the Northern part of France. She lost her life one fateful April day as the car in which she was a passenger tried to negotiate a curve much too fast, went out of control and began a series of rolls. Of the four occupants of the automobile hers was the only life lost. Though there is a lesson to be learned from this tragedy, never would this author wish to hurt the family of this young lady, nor to dishonor her memory. For that reason we will give her for now, the name of Yvette.

The photograph accompanying the newspaper article is touching as you see the white wooden cross planted on the roadside at the place where Yvette lost her life. There is a plaque attached to the cross, with her portrait, and a poem. Fresh flowers from family and friends appear on a regular basis to adorn the foot of this simple cross. And yet as you read the article you realize that this accident didn't have to happen, as they seldom do. For you see, Yvette almost did not take that fateful ride that evening. She was safe at home on that fresh spring day when some friends decided to spend the evening together. When she told her parents of her plans, her Father refused. After all, she had classes the next morning. This was no time to be out "joyriding", and besides, vacations weren't far away. As is often the case in such situations, the girl turned to her Mother for help, and found it, as her Father's wishes were quickly overridden and she was free to go. She kissed them goodbye and danced lightly out of the house. How could they know that this would be the last time they would see her alive?

As the Gendarmes awoke them in the early morning hours so began a life for this precious family that would never again be the same!

Sometimes accidents just happen. Sometimes they could have been avoided. We cannot help but grieve with this family in the loss of such a lovely and promising young daughter, even though we know that this life did not have to be lost and that little white cross did not have to find a place there along side the road. The Bible gives us counsel that would be good for us all to heed. There are Bible passages to help us, such as:

1. For our children and young people: *Ephesians 6:1-3, "Children, obey your parents in the Lord: for this is right. Honour thy Father and Mother; which is the first commandment with promise; that it may be well with thee, and thou mayest live long on the earth."*

2. For Fathers: *Ephesians 6:4, "And ye Fathers, provoke not your children to wrath: but bring them up in the nurture and admonition of the Lord."*

3. For the Moms and Dads who need to work together as a team: *Amos 3:3, "Can two walk together, except they be agreed?"*

Young people can take "no" as a valid answer. One parent does not have to override the other when there is a difference of opinion. And little white crosses do not have to adorn the sides of our roads!

THE POWER OF A PORTRAIT

S he was a lovely young lassie from the Scottish Highlands; trying to look beyond the wind swept mountains to the world beyond. Life there held little interest for a young lady with a head full of dreams such as she. Her widowed Mother worked long and hard to provide the basic necessities for the two of them, but this was not enough for her hungry heart. So she resolved to set out for Glasgow, the big city with its big attractions where a girl could make a place for herself, and even the tears in her Mother's eyes could not hold back this modern day prodigal daughter.

Much like the prodigal son in Luke 15, her joys were short lived. Her meager savings were quickly gone, and she soon found herself living in the most degraded condition, in the most squalid part of Glasgow, which had nothing to offer the wayward Highland lassie, except to rob her of her purity and pride. During this time never was there a passing moment when her Mother's heart and thoughts did not call out to her. Her Mother had no success in her numerous trips to Glasgow in search of her child, but an idea did come to her. The Midnight Mission was a home in Glasgow where young ladies in distress could take refuge, and find help and a safe place to sleep. This Mother easily received permission to post her own portrait in some of the rooms of the mission in the hopes that her daughter would one day pass that way, and be reminded of home and of the one there that still loved her.

Many young ladies did stop before that portrait, often moving on only after a tear and a sigh. One day another lady did stop before that appealing portrait as she recognized the face of the one that had cradled her childhood in love.

"Does this mean that my Mother has not forgotten me?" she asked herself. "She has not rejected her wayward child, or this portrait would not be hanging here on this wall," she thought. "She still thinks about me with affection!" The more she stared at her Mother's portrait the more it seemed her Mother's lips were whispering: "Come home! All is forgiven! I love you!"

Falling onto a nearby bench the young lady broke into a stream of tears and sobs that sprang from the depths of her blackened heart and soul. How she regretted the wasted years, and the squandered life! She knew there was only one way to turn, towards home. Packing her few ragged belongings into a small valise she made her way home, where she found her Mother's open arms, and the forgiveness on which she could build her life anew.

Prodigal son, prodigal daughter, is it not time for you to turn towards home and the Saviour that still loves you? You have left His way to follow the ways of the world, but the world has robbed you of everything of worth and value. The Bible paints a portrait of the unchanging love of God for you. Look deep into His compassionate face now and you will no doubt be able to see His lips whispering to you: "*Yea, I have loved thee with an everlasting love: therefore with lovingkindness have I drawn thee.*" *(Jeremiah 31:3)* Are you ready to make your way home now prodigal child, to the One that loved you enough to die for you? He is waiting for you, at the door of your heart!

THE OBSTINATE KING

Henri de Vic was nervous, very nervous. He was well known as one of the best clockmakers of all of France, but that knowledge was of little comfort to him that day as he journeyed to the Palace of the King to present to His Majesty a clock made under his orders. De Vic knew he had done a masterful job. He knew the clock was exquisitely beautiful and unquestionably accurate. So why such fear? De Vic had received the order for this clock from the King himself, Charles V, (1337-1380), and de Vic knew the King to be a very difficult person to please. Known as Charles "Le Sage", (Charles the Wise), the King fancied himself to be of extreme wisdom, and seldom missed a chance to display his wisdom, even when he was far from right on a matter. Often pretending to understand things he knew nothing about, he was still the King, and a King could require that he be called whatever he wished, and he insisted on being called Charles the Wise.

Charles V admired the clock with obvious pleasure, and why not? It was one of the most beautiful time-pieces ever presented to a King of France. The humble but masterful clockmaker had clearly poured his heart and soul into this endeavor. After a few moments the smile on the King's face turned somewhat more somber. Scrutinizing the clock ever more closely the King began to circle it, looking at the most infinites-imal detail. Obviously seeking some fault, some error with which to show his great wisdom, the King could find nothing. Nothing! Finally, with a glow of satis-faction he drew the attention of the clockmaker to the fact that on the face of the dial, the Roman Numeral for IV should have been IIII. De Vic made the mistake of saying: "Your Majesty is wrong!" Lightening shot from his eyes as Charles thundered out: "I am never wrong! Take the clock and return it when you have corrected this error!" And so, history tells us, began a tradition that can be seen today in our clocks and watches with this Roman Numeral being written IIII instead of IV, as it should be, reminding us of one King's remarkably obstinate wayward wisdom.

There is nothing wrong with wishing to be wise. The Bible even recommends it, such as in Proverbs 4:7, *"Wisdom is the principal thing; therefore get wisdom: and with all thy getting get understanding."* Or again, Proverbs 19:8, *"He that getteth wisdom loveth his own soul."*

There is however, a warning against getting the wrong kind of wisdom, built upon pride and the flesh. Proverbs 3:5-7 warns us: *"Trust in the Lord with all thine heart; and lean not unto thine own understanding. In all thy ways acknowledge Him, and He shall direct thy paths. Be not wise in thine own eyes: fear the Lord, and depart from evil."* The apostle Paul also tells us in Romans 12:16, *"Be not wise in your own conceits."*

The wisdom we need can only come from God. James 3:17 tells us: *"But the wisdom that is from above is first pure, then peaceable, gentle, and easy to be intreated, full of mercy and good fruits, without partiality, and without hypocrisy."* James 1:5 reminds us: *"If any of you lack wisdom, let him ask of God, that giveth to all men liberally, and upbraideth not; and it shall be given him."*

True wisdom from God is not obstinate, but humble. It is not ego centered, but truth centered.

True wisdom takes little credit for being right, but readily recognizes when it was in the wrong. May every morning of our lives find us humbly asking God for that wisdom that is from above, from God Himself, and we can be sure that it will be pure, peaceable, and gentle!

A SAVIOUR THAT KNOWS HOW TO SAVE

I t was meant to be a festive occasion, but it ended in death and tragedy. The day had started well enough for all involved in this small French town about half way between Paris and the Belgian border. For ten years now Jean (John, in French) and his wife Maryse had been enjoying their retirement after long years of hard work and raising their family of three boys and three girls. One of the daughters lived with her family a scant two miles from her parents' home. They saw each other often, such as on this sweltering August afternoon when the parents were invited over for a backyard barbecue. All went well, and great pleasure was had by all, until evening approached and Jean and Maryse needed to return home. The balmy evening invited the retired couple to walk the two miles home by way of a footpath that ran alongside a canal, bringing them almost to their own back door. They had taken this path many times before. The walk would do them good, so a wave of the hand, a last farewell, and off they set, never to be seen alive again.

It was the next morning that another walker spotted the first body near the banks of the river. The second body was found a few feet further away out in deeper water. Initial investigations have concluded that Maryse fell into the canal for reasons not yet determined. Jean, seeing the plight of his dear wife, plunged in to save her, but was unable to save either her, or himself. We can only imagine the horror he felt as he saw his wife slip into the dark waters. Listening only to his heart, he plunged.

Because of his age and the difficult circumstances he was unable to save either of them. What started out as a festive occasion ended with sorrow for a large family and brought consternation to the whole town.

Our hearts cannot help but be touched by this true story of human tragedy. But there is a greater tragedy! The tragedy of those seeking to offer salvation to the world when in reality they cannot save either the world, or themselves. History has been full of such "saviours". Many have presented themselves as "gods" offering eternal life to those that obeyed and followed them. Some were emperors, leading millions to futile death, and a Christless eternity. They were "saviours" that did not know how to save. Unlike those who choose to follow the Lord Jesus Christ, Who is certainly a Saviour that knows perfectly how to save!

Hebrews 7:25 tells us: *"Wherefore He is able to save them to the uttermost that come unto God by Him, seeing He ever liveth to make intercession for them."* We see here that not only is Christ able to save the repentant sinner, but He is able to save him to the "uttermost" which simply means "completely". Christ can save all of us, all the way. No partial salvation here! And there can be no other Saviour, for I Timothy 2:5 tells us: *"For there is one God, and one mediator between God and men, the man Christ Jesus."* In spite of his best intentions, man cannot save man. He cannot even save himself. Only Jesus Christ is the Saviour that knows how to save! Have you come to Him for salvation?

THE ART OF
THANKFULNESS

I have heard this story on several occasions, and
each time it seemed to be set in a different time,
in a different setting. A book that came into my hands
may have settled that question once and for all. To get
to the origin of this story we must go back in time to
the battlefields of France during the First World War.
A hastily set up camp had been prepared for men on
the move towards the front lines. Inside a makeshift
tent enlisted men and officers were enjoying a warm
meal. Little importance was put on rank as these tired
and hungry men sat down for this moment of respite.
A young member of the medical corps entered the
tent and sat down to eat. He then bowed his head,
and prayed a silent prayer of thanksgiving for his

meal. Though he did nothing to attract attention to himself, a few irreverent soldiers noticed his actions, and some muffled snickers could be heard.

At the head of the table sat a General, sullenly taking his meal with the weight of so many lives upon his shoulders. He could not help but notice the action of the young medic. A stern look from his eyes and the snickering ceased, and a hush settled under this humble tent. The young medic finished his prayer and looked up sheepishly when he realized all eyes were upon him.

—Young man, may I ask just exactly what you were doing? asked the General, without any sign of animosity or mockery.

—I was merely trying to make a distinction between myself and the animals, Sir! came the confident reply, though not without respect for his commanding officer.

The General did not seem to be vexed by this unique reply. Quite to the contrary.

—In that case soldier, would you please stand and say a word of prayer loud and clear for each one of us here? came the unexpected request from the General.

This was done, and in this way a word of thanksgiving was offered to God Almighty, and His name was properly honored.

We live in a day when the words, "Thank You" seem to have been lost from the vocabulary of so many people. People often feel that everything they receive is due them, so why say, "Thank You" when it is rightfully yours? A husband may not be thankful for the good wife that bears his name. Children may not be thankful for the good fortune they enjoy in having a nice home and decent parents. A worker may not appreciate his job, until he loses it. We often take our health for granted. But no doubt we are the most guilty when we forget to thank God for His great goodness towards us. The beasts of the field may not think to bow their heads to thank the God of Heaven for their provisions, but man should never fail to do so. We should be able to see the hand of God in every good thing that comes our way, and be thankful.

King David understood this when he said: *"Bless the Lord, O my soul; and all that is within me, bless His Holy Name. Bless the Lord, O my soul, and forget not all His benefits." (Psalm 103: 1-2)* The art of thanksgiving should be practiced daily, and the more we practice the better we will be at it. King David was thankful for all of the God sent benefits he saw in his life, and he thanked the Lord for them. And so should we all. Often!

A RELIGION FOR ALL WEATHERS

Tourists don't usually flock to the Cornwall coast of Western England, the victim of an unwarranted bad reputation. True, the rocky cliffs are often buffeted by thunderous storms coming in off the Celtic Sea to the West, but the climate is often mild, and the windswept moorlands are harsh, but inviting. The people of Cornwall are a hard working and generous people.

Those same storm battered cliffs also produce many beautiful harbors where one can find safety in the worst of times. In was in one of these harbors many years ago, that the faith and courage of the entire village was put to the test. For nearly a month the strong winds had been blowing in strongly from the land, making it possible to put their fishing vessels out to sea, but making it nearly impossible to return to port. With no fish being brought in many families were on the brink of bankruptcy, with local commerce also suffering. At last there was a break in the weather, but it was a Sunday morning. Though they rarely took to the sea on a Sunday, times were desperate, so a few men went down to their boats at the docks, with wives and children looking on.

"I'm sorry it's a Sunday, but times are hard", sighed one man, in excusing himself from this break with village tradition. "If I were not so poor, I wouldn't have to go", exclaimed another.

From the back of the gathering crowd an old fisherman stepped forward and in his familiar, weathered voice, proclaimed for all to hear: "Surely neighbors, you are not going to break God's laws with your 'buts' and 'ifs'. Mine's a religion for all weathers, fair and foul. This is the love of God, that ye keep His law. Remember the Sabbath day to keep it holy; that's the law friends. True, we are poor, but what of that? Better poor and have God's smile, than rich and have His frown. Go you that dare; but I never knew any good come of a religion that changed with the wind!"

Seeing the wisdom of these words the fishermen returned to their homes, and spent the day in prayer and praise. That same evening, just as they would have been returning to port had they set out to sea, a fierce storm sprang up and raged on for two days. On the third day the weather cleared and all ships were able to put out to sea, bringing in one of the greatest harvests seen in that area for many years. How happy they were to have reconsidered, and to have decided to have: "A religion for all weathers, fair and foul."

God promises this, to those that will trust Him, fair weather or foul: *"The Lord is nigh unto all them that call upon Him, to all that call upon Him in truth. He will fulfill the desire of them that fear Him: He also will hear their cry, and will save them." (Psalm 145: 18-19)*

Looking at the blustering winds and raging seas in our storms of life will only serve to discourage us. Looking unto the Master, brings calm!

THE CHILDHOOD
PRAYER OF MOZART

Wolfgang Amadeus Mozart, (1756-1791), was just a child when he invited his sister Frederika to go for a walk in the forest near their home in Salzburg, Austria. The two children enjoyed the singing of the birds and the babbling of the brook, but Wolfgang seemed preoccupied as they stopped for a moment in the shade of a large tree. Thus began a remarkable and true story.

The young Mozart said that the place would be a wonderful place to pray. Pray about what? About their parents who were poor and could barely feed the family. Their Father, Leopold, was constantly saddened to not be able to care properly for his family. Wolfgang felt they should pray for the help of God, and Frederika agreed, so there in their grassy woodland cathedral they knelt together and prayed aloud to God for Divine help for the needs of the family.

—"You know Frederika, he said as he rose from his knees, my soul is full of music. One day I am going to play before Kings. I will receive much money, and I will give it to our parents. We will live in a great house, and we will be happy!"

At this moment a hearty laugh jolted the two youngsters to attention as a dignified gentleman stepped from the bushes behind them. Walking by there by chance at that particular moment, he had stood in silent respect for the prayers of the two children. But the boasting of young Wolfgang was so amusing he could not refrain from laughing. Frederika came to her brother's defense.

—"My brother is very young, she propounded, but he plays marvelously well, and he is also a very good composer."

—"Yes, yes, I am quite sure he is", replied the gentleman courteously, not without a wry smile in the corner of his lips.

—"Come to my house this evening, said Mozart, and I will improvise for you!"

The stranger said he would be there, directions were given to their home, and the two youths hurried along to inform their parents of their new found friend that would be there in the evening.

That evening the house bustled with nervous activity, each one wondering if the woodland gentleman would really make an appearance. They all jumped as someone knocked at their humble door. Upon opening they were started to find men waiting to enter with baskets of groceries in their arms. As the food was placed upon the table Wolfgang and Frederika saw in this an answer to their youthful prayers. The young boy went to the piano and began to play, filling the humble abode with the majestic music that would eventually make Mozart a household name around the world. As Mozart played, the door opened softly as the children's gentleman friend slipped in. Leopold Mozart turned to greet their guest when he froze in his steps, for there before him he recognized Francois I, Emperor of Austria! The young Wolfgang had boasted he would one day play before Kings. Little did he know he would be doing so that very evening!

You may well know some of his major compositions, such as: Don Giovanni, The Magic Flute, or the

Marriage of Figaro, but did you know of his simple faith in his childhood prayers?

Listen to the wisdom of these words found in Psalm 70:5, *"For Thou art my hope, O Lord God: Thou art my trust from my youth."* The prayers of a child, or childlike prayers, both earn the respect and attention of God! Flowery words cannot mask a heart full of pride and sin. May our prayers be full of: worship towards God Himself, humility, simplicity, and faith!

THE LION OF LUCERNE

S hould you be able today to visit Lucerne, Switzerland it is said you would find an impressive statue of a lion, sculptured by the Swiss artist Ahorn from a model by the celebrated Danish sculptor Albert Bertel Thorwaldsen, (1770-1844). This lion, hewn out of solid rock and dedicated in 1821, stands 21 feet long and 18 feet high, and is transfixed by a broken spear. Although dying the lion is depicted as still trying to defend with its paw a shield bearing lilies, the emblem of France. The base of the statue contains this inscription in Latin: "Helvetiorum fidei ac virtuti", ("To the faithfulness and virtue of the Swiss"). The lion is a memorial from the Swiss people honoring the memory of the 26 officers and nearly 700 soldiers of the famous Swiss Guard who sacrificed their lives in the defense of Louis XVI and Marie-Antoinette during the French Revolution. What tragic set of circumstances brought about the deaths of these Swiss Guard members, inspiring the respect and admiration of their whole country? Their story is worth remembering, and their courage honored.

The Swiss Guard was instituted in the early 16th century when Swiss mercenaries were a prized fighting force in the armies of Europe. The most famous of these were those attached to the personal protection of the King and Queen of France. When the French Revolution began in the 1700's, Louis XVI and Marie-Antoinette were in their magnificent palace at Versailles. Because of the increasing violence, on October 6, 1789 they fled to their residential palace in the heart of Paris, the Tuileries Palace, where they hid out along with nearly the entire National Assembly. An attempt to escape on June 21, 1790 failed as the insurgent crowds became more and more threatening. The Royal family, hiding in the Assembly Room, counted on the French Army as well as the Swiss Guard to hold off the swelling crowds in the streets. One should not be fooled by the colorful and frilly uniforms of the Swiss Guard, supposedly designed by Michelangelo, for the Swiss

Guard were some of the most courageous and formidable warriors of Europe, as the following events would soon prove.

On August 10, 1792 thousands of protesters filled the streets of Paris seeking the heads of Louis XVI and his Queen, Marie-Antoinette. As the enraged mob stormed the Tuileries Palace the French Guard deserted their posts and fled, leaving the Swiss Guard to stand alone. Listening only to their courage and honor, and loyal to their given word, stand they did. As the invading mob rushed in the Swiss Guard held their ranks and fought, but the sheer numbers of the insurgent forces were too great for even them. As the dust of battle settled dozens of protesters lay dead, but the maddened crowd had clubbed and hacked to death all 26 officers and nearly 700 soldiers of the Swiss Guard. Their courage inspired the making of the Lion of Lucerne; their valor has solicited the honor and respect of the entire Swiss people.

It is absolutely normal to pay respect where respect is due. Does not the Bible tell us: *"Render therefore to all their dues: tribute to whom tribute is due; custom to whom custom; fear to whom fear; honour to whom honour." (Romans 13:7)* It is befitting to see in nearly every country solemn monuments honoring those who have died in the line of duty, be it in military service, or as Policemen, Firemen, or other places of public and noble service. Honoring those who died for us should come naturally for a Christian as we think of the Lord Jesus Christ, for we can say: *"Worthy is the Lamb that was slain to receive power, and riches, and wisdom, and strength, and honour, and glory, and blessing." (Revelation 5:12)*

GOD DOESN'T DO IT AS MAN DOES

Anumber of years ago the owner of a hunting lodge high in the mountains of Scotland decided it was time for a complete make-over of his lodge. He spared no expense. The lodge was modernized, made more comfortable and far more beautiful than ever before. The eve of the new hunting season found the lodge full of hunters enjoying a boisterous evening meal. One such reveler, seeking to open a bottle of carbonated mineral water clumsily sent a burst of water surging towards a large mural painting covering the entire wall behind the dining table. The room grew silent as all eyes watched the bubbling water begin to run down the length of the painting. The paint had begun to run, and the painting was ruined. The owner sat in stunned silence, as each man slipped off quietly to his room. The next morning the men left just as quietly for their hunting stations, leaving the lodge owner to his grief.

One hunter however, stayed behind. When all were gone he went to his baggage and took out a complete set of artistry equipment. Everything an experienced painter would need was there. After cleaning the mural painting he set to work. And work he did, changing the nature and the theme of the painting completely. Taking away the hideous blotches and working with speed and accuracy he soon produced one of the most beautiful scenes of the Scottish Highlands you would ever hope to see. A majestic waterfall came cascading down between two large rocks as a young deer looked on. The scene was so realistic that the returning hunters could only stand and gaze in awe. For you see, the painter was none other than world renowned artist Sir Edwin Lanseer, one of the foremost natural life painters England has ever produced. The first mural painting had been done by a very good artist; the second by a great master! A master that would not give up on a disfigured painting.

How wonderful it is that God does not give up either on disfigured works! A child of God is a wonderful work of grace, that can easily find himself disfigured by sin. How easy it is to let sin in, and lose the beauty we once had in Christ! Did you once walk close to the Lord, but not now? Were you once faithful to God, His Word, and His House, but no more? Did you once strive to keep yourself free from sin, but sin has now become your constant companion? While others can only walk away shaking their heads in sadness and disgust, there is One that stays behind with you to do a work of grace in your life, if you will let Him.

In Matthew 12:20 Jesus quotes Isaiah 42:3 when He says: *"A bruised reed shall He not break, and smoking flax shall He not quench, till He send forth judgment unto victory."* The smoking flax speaks of the smoking wick in an old oil lamp. It used to work properly, but not now. Instead of tossing it aside, as man would, God takes the dirtied vessel, cleanses it, and trims the wick, making it fit again for service. That is the way God works. Man rejects, God repairs. Man destroys, God re-employs. God does not give up on His wayward children. He will cleanse and purity you, if you will only let Him!

THE PRAYER THAT JESUS REFUSED TO PRAY

Did you realize that there was at least one prayer in the Bible that Jesus refused to pray? In a way that is somewhat hard to imagine, especially when you notice that it was an issue that concerned the well being of His disciples.

We know that Jesus could have prayed any prayer He wanted, but He could not allow himself to pray this one. We find that story in John 17:15, where Jesus is praying a prayer of intercession for His disciples, asking the Father to help them and be with them, knowing that He was only hours away from the crucifixion. He would soon leave His disciples behind as He returned to His rightful place in Heaven. Here is the prayer that Jesus refused to pray, in that verse 15, saying: *"I pray not that Thou shouldest take them out of the world, but that Thou shouldest keep them from evil."*

Most of us would not have thought to pray that way. Knowing the trials and hard times awaiting the disciples after the departure of Christ, moved with pity for them, the average Christian would have prayed for them to be spared the terrible days of trial and torture to come. But Jesus did not do that. Instead,

He prayed just the opposite: *"I pray not that Thou shouldest take them out of the world"*. Jesus actually asked the Father to leave them in the world, and yet to be with them, and help them as they faced the difficult days ahead. There is a very good reason for this. Perhaps the following true story will help us under- stand.

Many years ago London was being ravaged by a terrible epidemic that had claimed thousands of lives, and left thousands more on the brink of death. A wealthy landowner and influential figure, Lord Craven, decided to leave London for the countryside where the risks of contagion were less likely. His luxury automobile was waiting at the door of his sumptuous home as he had his servants carry out his baggage. As he was waiting by the door for this to be done he overheard one of his servants of African descent, turn and whisper to Lord Craven's chauffeur: "Since Milord is leaving London to flee the danger of contagion, I suppose that his God is a God that only lives in the country, and not in town."

Lord Craven could not help overhearing this remark, and he was touched in his heart and soul. He had often spoken of his faith in God, and encouraged others to place their trust in the Almighty, and yet here he was fleeing to the country-side, as if his God was too small to protect him in the city. He had his baggage returned to their places in his room, where he fell on his knees in prayer asking God to forgive him for his unbelief and failure to trust Him in the sickness infested city as much as he thought he could in the fresh countryside.

We need to take this lesson one important step further. Jesus wanted us here for a very good reason: To carry the Gospel to the multitudes still without Christ and without hope in this world. If God had taken us out of the world immediately after our salvation, our witness to the lost and dying would have been lost. Later on in this same prayer, Jesus prayed: "Neither pray I for these alone, but for them also which shall believe on me through their words."

(John 17:20) Yes, this was one prayer that Jesus could pray. The world needs us to hear the glorious Gospel of Christ, and we need this honor to serve Him, laying up for ourselves treasures in Heaven that we will one day be able to lay at His feet. May we never forget why Jesus wanted us left here below!

FROM DESERTER
TO HERO

It is shortly before 5 AM, June 29, 1940 on this French Military airbase in the Algerian port town of Oran. Under the cover of darkness 14 shadowy figures glide furtively from hiding place to hiding place as they try to reach 3 airplanes waiting in silence near the runway. They must be careful not to be caught, for they are deserters from the French Air Force, and as such their lives are at stake. But flee they must, for France has just capitulated to the German occupational army, and all French military has been ordered to lay down their weapons. These men are not deserting to flee the war, but in order to fight for their country. One of these men, René Mouchotte wrote this: "I wish to leave for England. Because my country has rejected me as a fighter, I shall still fight for him, in spite of him, without him!"

And so it is that 6 of these men take place in a Goéland, 6 more in another, and the other 2 in a much smaller Simoun. The Renault motors roar into life, but there is no time for doing a checklist as the 3 airplanes make for the runway before sleepy guards can get off a shot. Their 300 mile journey to British held Gibraltar has begun. Joining the British Royal Air Force in England they brought honor to their country as some of the finest fighters to come out of those dark days. Few of them survived the war. René Mouchotte went on to become commander of a whole fighter wing, earning the respect of all that knew him. His sense of devotion was unequaled, his bravery unquestioned, often leading his group of 24 Spitfires against formations of over 200 German aircraft. His last flight came on August 27, 1943 when his plane was brought down during battle in northern France. His body was later found washed up on the shore near Middelkerge, Belgium.

All of England was shaken by the news of the death of the valiant French fighter. René Mouchotte had flown in 332 military operations against the enemy, totaling more than 1743 hours of combat flying time. He was so highly respected as a leader that French ace Pierre Clostermann once said of him: "The kind of man you can die with, without argument, almost with pleasure!" France did not forget her fallen son, bringing his body back to Paris on November 10, 1949 for a nationally honored funeral with burial at the honored "Les Invalides". The Distinguished Flying Cross, La Croix de Guerre, and other highest honors were rightfully bestowed upon this noble hero, once considered a deserter by those that did not understand.

The Bible says that other men and women have often been misunderstood, considered heroes by some and deserters by others. Speaking of the "heroes of faith" Hebrews 11:37-38 describes them thusly: *"They were stoned, they were sawn asunder, were tempted, were slain with the sword: they wandered about in sheepskins and goatskins; being destitute, afflicted, tormented; of whom the world was not worthy!"* The world did not find them worthy? And yet they were found worthy in the sight of God, who will say to each of His children in that glad and glorious eternal day: *"Well done, thou good and faithful servant!"* *(Matthew 25:21)* It matters not what the world may say, as long as we find favor with the Father!

THE DICE OF DEATH

Would you go to a museum just to see a pair of gambling dice? Not many people would, but it seems that should you visit the Museum of Arts in Berlin, Germany you will find a simple pair of gambling dice. Here is the astounding story behind this very commonplace set of gambler's dice.

This story begins over 200 years ago as we find the whole town in turmoil after the brutal assassination of the beautiful young daughter of Walther, the well known weapons manufacturer. Two soldiers were quickly arrested. Alfred and Raoul were both known to have had romantic interests in the young lady and it seemed their bitter rivalry had pushed one of them, in a fit of jealousy and rage, to commit this murder. One of them was no doubt the guilty party, but which one? Neither would confess. They both claimed innocence.

Torture, a common practice in those days, failed to produce a confession from either man. In spite of great investigation, not a convincing shred of evidence could be brought forth. The Magistrate, feeling public and political pressure to produce a convictable culprit, found himself in a serious dilemma. What could he do to determine the guilty man? He remembered a practice that had long since been abandoned by the German people, as it was by most other civilized nations, the use of a simple pair of dice. Seeing no other alternative the Magistrate determined that Alfred and Raoul would lay their lives on the line by the way of a roll of gambler's dice. And so it came to pass.

At the appointed time the Magistrate entered the packed courtroom. The person rolling the highest number on the dice would be declared innocent. The other would be executed. Raoul, the haughty and arrogant one, was chosen to go first. He had few friends in the audience. The tension was palpable as Raoul slowly shook the dice in his hands and gave them a roll. Gasps were heard everywhere as a double six came up. Impossible to do better than that! How could it be that he was the innocent one and the quiet, timid Alfred was the murderer?

Alfred approached the dice on the table, his legs nearly failing him. Those standing nearby could hear Alfred whisper: "Oh, come to my aide Eternal God; you know that I am innocent!" In his fear and trembling Alfred threw the dice with great force. As they rebounded off the wall a snap was heard. The uproar was stupendous as every eye looking on saw that one of the dice had snapped in two, showing a double six, just as Raoul had produced. But on the other half of the broken dice was a one, just as you will find on any set of dice. Six plus six, plus one! That makes 13! Against all odds Alfred had beaten the seemingly perfect score of 12 thrown by Raoul. The magistrates could only agree that "fate" had brought justice to this case. Raoul would be executed. As if struck by lightening Raoul collapsed to the floor, and in a semi-conscious murmur could be heard to say that he had been found out, yes, he was the killer!

God does want justice to be done, and though justice is often thwarted here on earth, the truth will always be known before God's throne of judgment in heaven. Ecclesiastes 12:13-14 offers a sobering thought for all those who think they have "gotten away with it" in man's court of law: *"Let us hear the conclusion of the whole matter: Fear God, and keep His commandments: for this is the whole duty of man. For God shall bring every work into judgment, with every secret thing, whether it be good, or whether it be evil."*

Don't base your future on a risky roll of the dice, but rather in the grace of God that will direct you in paths of righteousness for His name's sake!

A MOTHER'S PRAYERS

Many years ago, on the water's edge of a small British port town, there stood the modest cottage of a widow, whose sea captain husband had been lost at sea. She lived there in extreme modesty with her two sons, 10 and 6 years old. It was a terrible struggle just to make a living, but in it all she never failed to train her two young boys, "in the way they should go". However, at the early age of 12 her older son, William, found a position as an apprentice on a large brig, and prepared to set sail. Her heart breaking within her the weary widow at last gave her consent, offering her departing son a Bible, and the promise of her prayers for him. He in turn promised to read that Bible and give himself to prayer, a promise he never kept.

For a short while the well intended boy seemed to keep his promise, but the sneers and jeers of the wicked crew soon pushed that promise to the back of his mind. It was just a matter of time until he too found himself indulging in the darkest of sins, as his vessel put into ports around the world, where he spent his leisure moments in bars and brothels. It was with this burden upon his heart that he now stood on the forward deck of his ship looking towards the approaching coasts of England. He had been gone for several years, but he would be home tonight. His steps quickened as he hurried from the port across town to where the little cottage stood, but as he approached that cherished door a strange apprehension overtook him. All was quiet and silence. No light could be seen, no sound could be heard. His knocking and his calling could produce no response. Shortly, a neighbor lady saw him standing there, and drew near. She soon realized that she had standing before her the long, lost, prodigal William. In a moment's time she had explained that the younger boy had died about a year ago after a terrible bout with a fever. The battle in taking care of her young son was too much for the dear widow, who died of exhaustion and she too had just been buried. Asking William to wait, the lady hurried to her cottage and returned with a letter addressed to William, written by his dear Mother just days before her passing. Choking back tears, this is what William read:

"My dearest, only son! When this reaches you I shall be no more. Your little brother has gone before me, and I cannot but hope and believe that he was prepared. I have fondly hoped that I should once more have seen you on the shores of mortality, but this hope is now relinquished. I have followed you by my prayers through all your wanderings. There is but one thing which gives me pain at dying; and that is, my dear William, that I must leave you in this wicked world, as I fear unreconciled to your Maker! I am too feeble to say more. My glass is run. As you visit the sods which cover my dust, oh, remember that you too must soon follow. Farewell, the last breath of your Mother will be spent in praying for you, that we may meet above!"

Dear reader friend, have the prayers of a Godly Mother gone so far unheeded in your own life? Have you strayed far from the Godly teaching you learned in your early days at your Mother's knees? The reading of this letter brought young William to his senses, and to salvation in Christ. The rest of his life was devoted to Christ. Is it time for you to come to the same place of repentance and salvation? Do so today!

THE MURDERER'S MESSAGE

This sultry day of 1912 found Miguel Vallespy slowly walking the streets of Rosario, Argentina with his head down, his shoulders slumped and a lazy shuffle to his feet. His heart was heavy as he thought of the terrible events of his past life, for you see Miguel was not from Argentina, but Spain. Years earlier he had left his native Spain for the small town of Coursan in the South of France, just a few kilometers from Carcassonne, where work was plentiful, wages were profitable and life was agreeable. Unfortunately Miguel carried within his breast a tempestuous heart, ready to be set aflame at the slightest provocation. Miguel had been guilty of having attempted murder on four individuals, and having killed another. Fearing the death penalty for murder he fled France for Argentina in 1907, hearing later that he had been tried "in absentia" and found guilty. There was no going back. Or was there?

Lost in his thoughts Miguel came upon a large crowd that had gathered to hear a street preacher proclaiming the love and pardon of God for all sinners. The Word of God went straight to the heart of this meandering murderer, and brought Miguel to his knees in a sincere prayer for forgiveness for his sins. In turning to Christ he knew he was beginning a new life, but what would he do about the "old business" still on his heart's ledger? He decided to return to France and deliver himself to the French authorities. He had to work long and hard to save up enough money for this one way trip to what could be his execution, but on May 7, 1913, after a brief stop in Spain to say farewell to his sister, Miguel walked into the Police Station in Carcassonne and turned himself in. His court appointed lawyer could not understand that all Miguel wanted to do was to recognize in court his guilt of murder, to tell of the grace of God that had saved him, and to ask forgiveness of his victim's brother who would be there in court. The courtroom was abuzz with amazement. The tension was palpable.

As Miguel began to speak hearts were touched. There was sincerity in his voice, a look of authenticity on his face. He explained how Christ has saved and changed him, of his eternal regrets for the harm he had done. In tears he turned to his victim's brother asking for his forgiveness for his crime. The jury took little time in deliberation. There was only one verdict possible: Miguel was acquitted. He was not declared innocent; he was declared pardoned! Amidst the tears and applause of those present, Miguel was able to walk out a free man. Returning to Coursan, the town of his crime, and now the town of his new life, Miguel lived the Christian life and carried a clear testimony for Christ until his death a number of years later.

Miguel has a message for us today. It is the same message he met on the streets of Rosario in Argentina that saved his soul and changed his life: *"Blessed are they whose iniquities are forgiven, and whose sins are covered. Blessed is the man to whom the Lord will not impute sin." (Romans 4:7-8)* Miguel wanted everyone to hear the message of salvation and forgiveness in Christ, the only way for the weight to be lifted from the heart, and the soul set eternally free. Have you heard this message today?

CROSSING OVER
TO THE OTHER SIDE

This true story has been told before, but should it be new to you I have no doubt that it will soon become one of your favorites. It is a story of comfort and compassion that also prepares us Scripturally for the time when we or our loved ones must pass over from this life into eternity.

This story takes us back a few years ago to the British countryside where we find a husband and his wife walking silently along a dusty trail through fields and pastures. Their little daughter had just died. She was their one and only child, and the Mother was inconsolable. Their faith in God didn't seem to be enough to see them through this unfathomable heartache, and though his arms were so often tenderly about the shoulders of his grieving wife, and his words few but full of compassion, the husband knew that only God could provide the soothing balm of heart and soul that they both needed.

Rounding a bend in this pastoral path the young couple saw in the fields before them a shepherd trying to get his flock of sheep to cross a fast running but narrow brook. The rippling sounds of the running water caused the sheep to be frightened. None would cross, much to the perplexity of the shepherd. His faithful sheepdog barking and nudging from behind the flock could get them to approach the noisy water's edge, but none would venture putting in the first hoof. What could he do? The husband and wife sat down on the hillside to see how the bewildered shepherd would solve this dilemma. They needn't wait long.

The shepherd picked up an old wooden plank found laying there, and placed it across a narrow stretch of the stream. Then, stepping into the midst of his flock he came to mama ewe with her tiny lamb beside her. Taking the lamb in his strong arms he stepped towards the plank. He could hear the bleating of the mother for her young one as he stopped at the edge of the plank, waiting for her to make her way through the flock to his heels. Every sheep in the flock had its eyes fixed on the ewe, on the shepherd, and on the lamb. Then, stepping slowly onto the plank the shepherd crossed over, the young one still calling for his mama. The mother was so afraid. The rippling of the water was still frightening as she hesitated just an instant, before maternal love pushed her forward onto the sagging plank and then quickly to her baby on the other side. The shepherd set the lamb down before the mother, and soon their joyous peals of reunion sounded like a trumpet call to the other sheep who took courage as they filed across the wooden pathway, until all the flock was safely over to the other side.

The grieving husband and wife watching this pastoral scene turned and looked silently at each other. No words were necessary as they realized that God had given them the answer they needed. Their precious daughter did not go off, "into the great unknown" in some precarious or vague fashion. They could see now how the Lord Himself, the Great Shepherd, had come and had taken their little one in His great arms, and had carried her safely across to "the other side". And in doing so He had also shown them the way they too would follow one day as they would find the Saviour and their little one waiting for them on eternity's distant shore. Does this not cause Mark 4:35 to take on new meaning for us as we read: *"When the even was come, He saith unto them, Let us pass over unto the other side"*.

The key to this verse is no doubt the word "US" as the Saviour crosses over with His disciples to the other side, just as each child of God will do some day, cradled safely in the arms of Jesus!

THE MESSAGE OF THE MIDDAY MOON

My wife and I had been driving since early that morning. It was now just past noon as we headed towards a high pass in the Vosges mountains in Eastern France. Alsace was just on the other side of those mountains as was the road leading us to a Bible Conference in which I was to participate. The sun was shining brightly, the sky was a radiant blue, and the road twisted and turned lazily as we made our way to the summit, still some ways in the distance. That was when we saw it. Coming around a bend in the road the nose of our automobile seemed to be pointing skyward, and there straight ahead hanging low in the sky was the moon. Large, full rounded and of an immaculate silver, it was a majestic sight. After a moment of silent awe I spoke to my wife of how unique it was to see the moon so clearly at midday.

I remembered what the Bible had to say about the moon and why it is primarily a denizen of the night. I remembered how God, on the fourth day of creation, *"Made two great lights; the greater light to rule the day, and the lesser light to rule the night."* *(Genesis 1:16)* If the moon was to rule the night what was he doing here at midday? I could understand the message of the midnight moon, but what was the message of the midday moon? The sun speaks of God's accompaniment as we go through life, giving us light and life. The night speaks of the hard times that often come along in life, and the moon is there in those dark hours to remind us that God is still with us and that the night will not last forever. God is never far away, just as the moon reminds us of the coming dawn. The midnight moon brings a message of hope and courage but what is the message of the midday moon, if there really is one?

I later noticed Isaiah 60:20 in my Bible. What a wonderful promise we find here! *"Thy sun shall no more go down; neither shall thy moon withdraw itself: for the Lord shall be thine everlasting light, and the days of thy mourning shall be ended."* Do you see it? "Thy sun shall no more go down; neither shall thy moon withdraw itself." The arrival of the sun will not chase the moon away. They shall dwell together in the heavens just as my wife and I witnessed on that exceptional spring day. We see this in Scriptures in Revelations 21:23 as we read: *"And the city had no need of the sun, neither of the moon, to shine in it: for the glory of God did lighten it, and the Lamb is the light thereof."*

The message of the midday moon is simply that the day will come when the moon will no longer be needed for the night, for there will be no more night in Heaven. The midday moon brings a message of hope as we stand for eternity with our faces to the sun, and our backs to the darkness forever. What a glorious message it is!

There was a time when I lived with unspeakable joy because the young lady I loved the most in all the world had accepted to wear our engagement ring, accepting to join her life to mine. But after months of waiting we stood before the minister and I placed another ring on her finger, her wedding ring. Both rings were of great importance to me and brought me much joy, but since our wedding day I have something much more important than rings, I have her, my wife, the love of my life! The rings were a promise from the one that loved me, bringing me unending joy. Reader friend, have you joined yourself unto Christ, that loved you enough to die for you?

Printed in the United States
132813LV00001BA/118-579/P

9 781606 479537